I0500435

A NATIONAL SECURITY STRATEGY FOR A GLOBAL AGE

THE WHITE HOUSE
DECEMBER 2000

Contents

Preface

As we enter the new millennium, we are blessed to be citizens of a country enjoying record prosperity, with no deep divisions at home, no overriding external threats abroad, and history's most powerful military ready to defend our interests around the world. Americans of earlier eras may have hoped one day to live in a nation that could claim just one of these blessings. Probably few expected to experience them all; fewer still all at once.

Our success is cause for pride in what we've done, and gratitude for what we have inherited. But the most important matter is what we now make of this moment. Some may be tempted to believe that open markets and societies will inevitably spread in an era of expanding global trade and communications, or assume that our wealth and power alone will protect us from the troubles of the outside world. But that approach falls for the old myth of an "outside" world, and ignores the defining features of our age: the rise of interdependence. More than ever, prosperity and security in America depend on prosperity and security around the globe. In this age, America can advance its interests and ideals only by leading efforts to meet common challenges. We must deploy America's financial, diplomatic and military resources to stand up for peace and security, promote global prosperity, and advance democracy and human rights around the world.

This demands strengthening our alliances with Europe and Asia, and adapting them to meet emerging challenges. Our alliances in Europe and Asia are stronger because they are organized to advance a permanent set of shared interests, rather than to defeat a single threat. We must continue working with our allies towards a peaceful, democratic, undivided Europe, with NATO as a deterrent to new conflict and a magnet for new democracies. In Asia, we must build on strategic alliance with Japan to define new approaches to post-Cold War threats. And, we must enhance cooperation with South Korea as we encourage North Korea's emergence from isolation and continue to diminish the missile threat.

Just as we strengthen our alliances, we must build principled, constructive, clear-eyed relations with our former adversaries Russia and China. We must be mindful of threats to peace while also maximizing chances that both Russia and China move toward greater internal openness, stability and prosperity, seizing on the desire of both countries to participate in the global economy and global institutions, insisting that both accept the obligations as well as the benefits of integration. With Russia, that means continuing our work to reduce the nuclear danger, to assure strategic stability, and to define its future role in Europe, while supporting the emergence of democratic institutions and the rule of law. With China, that means continuing to press for adherence to nonproliferation standards and peaceful dialogue with Taiwan, while holding Chinese leaders to the conditions of entry into the WTO, which offer the best hope of internal reform.

To protect the peace and promote security, we must work to resolve conflicts before they escalate and harm vital U.S. interests. In the 1990s, the United States has been actively engaged in seeking peace in the Middle East, in the Balkans, between Greece and Turkey, between India and Pakistan, in Northern Ireland, between Peru and Ecuador, and Eritrea and Ethiopia. These efforts, undertaken in partnership with friends and allies, help to avert wider conflicts that might endanger global stability, ease humanitarian catastrophes, while adding moral authority to America's might in the world. American overwhelming power and influence is far less likely to breed resentment if it is used to advance the cause of peace.

We also must identify and address new national security challenges, accentuated by new technology and open borders. We have identified a new security agenda that addresses contemporary threats such as the proliferation of nuclear, chemical and biological weapons, terrorism, and international crime. New efforts must continue to build on initiatives such as the extension of the Nonproliferation Treaty, the containment of nations seeking to acquire and use weapons of mass destruction, increased antiterrorism cooperation, stepped up efforts to combat trafficking in drugs, arms, and human- beings, and our first-ever national strategy for cybersecurity. Our new security agenda recognizes that in a global age, threats to America do not simply come from determined enemies and deadly weapons. Our efforts to curb global warming through the Kyoto protocol are vital to protect America from a future of rising sea levels and economic disruption. Our leadership in the international fight against infectious diseases, especially HIV/AIDS, is critical to defeat a threat that kills massively, crosses frontiers and destabilizes whole regions.

Finally, there can be no security where there is no hope of prosperity. We must continue to promote the spread of global markets in ways that advance economic growth, honor our values, and help alleviate economic disparity. We must build on the creation of the WTO, and of NAFTA, on the passage of PNTR for China, on extending trade preferences to nations in Africa and the Caribbean Basin, and on the nearly 300 trade agreements we have signed that have contributed to the longest U.S. economic expansion in history. At the same time, we must understand that trade, by itself, is not enough to lift the most desperate nations out of poverty or prevent the world from becoming bitterly divided between haves and have nots. That's why we have led in promoting the HIPC initiative to provide deeper debt reduction for countries with unsustainable debt burdens, and placed global development issues at the forefront of the international agenda.

More than 50 years ago, Harry Truman said: "We are in a position now of making the world safe for democracy, if we don't crawl in a shell and act selfish and foolish." He believed that in the wake of our triumph in World War II, America had the ability and a responsibility to shape world events, so that we would not be shaped by them. Truman was right, and the historical forces he saw then have only intensified since the Cold War.

The ability to assure global security, shared prosperity and freedom is beyond the power of any one nation. But the actions of many nations often follow from the actions of one. America today has power and authority never seen before in the history of the world. We must continue use it, in partnership with those who share our values, to seize the opportunities and meet the challenges of a global age.

William J. Clinton

I.   Fundamentals of the Strategy

Goals of the Engagement Strategy

Since the end of the Cold War, the United States and its allies have developed a position of extraordinary strength. As the last decade of the 20th century unfolded, the United States sought to use that strength wisely and in a manner consistent with the fundamental values and ideals on which our republic was founded. The world is undergoing an accelerating process of globalization in which technology is developing exponentially; information is exchanged around the globe cheaply and instantaneously; economies are increasingly interdependent; borders are more porous; people seek political and economic freedoms; and groups seek expression of their ethnic identity. Some of these trends add to our strength and security. Others present new challenges. All entail great transformation and prescribe new imperatives for defining our Nation's role in this rapidly changing era.

In a democracy, a nation's foreign policy and security strategy must serve the needs of the people. At the dawn of the 21st century, our world is very different from that of our Founding Fathers, yet the basic objectives in the preamble to the Constitution remain timeless:

> *provide for the common defence, promote the general welfare, and secure the blessings of liberty to ourselves and our posterity.*

The changes we have seen in the last decade do not alter these fundamental purposes. They merely blur the dividing line between domestic and foreign policy and heighten the imperative for a cohesive set of active U.S. efforts, both at home and abroad, to pursue three modern day goals derived from the preamble's objectives: **enhancing security at home and abroad, promoting prosperity, and promoting democracy and human rights.** To accomplish these three goals in an ever-shrinking world, we have developed a series of policies, now recognized as the elements of our strategy for engagement.

Elements of the Strategy

Shaping the International Environment

A primary element of our strategy of engagement has been to help fashion a new international system that promotes peace, stability, and prosperity. This has involved remolding and shaping both sides of the Cold War bipolar system. It has meant both **adapting our alliances and encouraging the reorientation of other states, including former adversaries.**

The United States has led the transformation of what were defensive entities into proactive instruments for meeting post-Cold War challenges. Under U.S. leadership, NATO -- our most important Cold War alliance -- has formally revised its strategic concept, successfully ended aggression in Bosnia and Kosovo, and brought new members into the Alliance while holding out the prospect of further enlargement. It has increasingly pursued new initiatives and missions such as the Partnership for Peace (PFP) and peacekeeping operations with partners to help stabilize the continent. New dialogue between historic adversaries interested in joining NATO has helped to reconcile several long-standing disputes among countries in the region. Further challenges exist, but the signs of progress and nature of the changes are encouraging.

Other important security arrangements we forged in the Cold War remain strong in the post-Cold War world. For instance, in 1997 the United States and Japan revised their guidelines for defense cooperation. Our security commitments to the Republic of Korea and Australia also remain strong, as do our defense relations with Thailand and the Philippines, and new security cooperation exists with our friends in the Persian Gulf region.

Nations with whom we had been philosophically opposed during much of the Cold War are in the process of tremendous political and economic change. Our engagement with these states over the last eight years has been focused on encouraging them to undertake important political and economic reforms while at the same time dissuading them from regressing into confrontational relationships. Our efforts with the most populous of these nations -- China and Russia -- have been intended to offer opportunities and incentives for proactive participation, while also encouraging them to be responsible members of the world community. This means progress in respecting the rights of individuals and nations in areas as diverse as the environment, humanitarian issues, the rule of law, and economic fairness. While the outcome of transformation in these nations is not altogether certain, our engagement has had a positive impact on both regional and global stability.

The United States has sought to strengthen the post-Cold War international system by **encouraging democratization, open markets, free trade, and sustainable development.** These efforts have produced measurable results. The number of democracies, as a percentage of world states, has increased by 14% since 1992. For the first time in history, over half of the world's population lives under democratic governance. Our national security is a direct beneficiary of democracy's spread, as democracies are less likely to go to war with one another, more likely to become partners for peace and security, and more likely to pursue peaceful means of internal conflict resolution that promote both intrastate and regional stability.

The globalization of trade and investment, spurred by new technologies, open borders, and increasingly open societies, is a critical aspect of the 21st century world. United States efforts to expand trade and investment with both traditional and new trading partners fuel growth in our economy. United States efforts to extend market reforms to former adversaries and neutrals also enhance our security by increasing economic cooperation, empowering reformers, and promoting openness and democracy overseas. Economic freedoms routinely facilitate political freedoms. In addition to these opportunities, economic globalization also presents its proponents with tough challenges, such as assisting countries that embrace but are nonetheless left behind by the dynamics of globalization or working with countries that reject these dynamics for fear of losing their cultural or national identity.

Preventing conflict has been a hallmark of U.S. foreign policy under a strategy of engagement. All over the world, the United States has selectively used diplomatic means, economic aid, military presence, and deterrence as tools for promoting peace. We also assist other countries to develop their own defense capabilities through our foreign assistance and security assistance programs. In doing so, we have focused on the threats and opportunities most relevant to our interests as well as our values, and applied our resources where we can make the greatest difference.

Responding to Threats and Crises

The persistence of major interstate conflict has required us to maintain the means for **countering potential regional aggressors.** Long-standing tensions and territorial division on the Korean peninsula and territorial ambitions in the Persian Gulf currently define the main tenets of this requirement. For the foreseeable future, the United States, preferably in concert with allies, must have the capability to deter -- and if that fails, to defeat -- large-scale, cross-border aggression in two distant theaters in overlapping time frames.

Globally, as a result of more porous borders, rapid changes in technology, greater information flow, and the potential destructive power within the reach of small states, groups, and individuals, the United States finds itself **confronting new threats** that pose strategic challenges to our interests and values. These include the potential use and continued proliferation of weapons of mass destruction (WMD) and their means of delivery, proliferation of small arms and light weapons, threats to our information/cyber security, international migrant smuggling and trafficking in persons, and the ability to disrupt our critical infrastructure. As a result, defense of the homeland against WMD terrorism has taken on a new importance, making coordinated Federal, state, and local government efforts imperative. The Domestic Preparedness Program has received significant resources to address immediate threats to our security. Ongoing efforts on National Missile Defense are developing the capability to defend the fifty states against a limited missile attack from states that threaten international peace and security. Prevention remains our first line of defense to lessen the availability of weapons of mass destruction being sought by such aggressor nations. To that end, we continue to work with Russia to control possible leakage of former Soviet nuclear, chemical, and biological weapons materials and expertise to proliferant states.

We are also vigorously pursuing a strengthening of the Nuclear Non-Proliferation Treaty, the Chemical and Biological Weapons Conventions, the Missile Technology Control Regime, and entry into force of the Comprehensive Nuclear Test Ban Treaty at the earliest possible time. Other persistent threats to our security in peacetime include international terrorism, drug trafficking, other organized crime, and environmental degradation. The United States has made great strides in restructuring its national security apparatus to address new threats with diplomatic, economic, and military tools.

Fragmentation of a number of states, which helped lead to the collapse of the Cold War's bipolar alignment, has caused turmoil within several regions of the world. This turmoil, a result of re-awakened ethnic and religious divisions and territorial ambitions, has reignited old conflicts and resulted in substantial bloodshed. U.S. leadership in **steering international peace and stability operations** has restored and maintained peace in a number of locations. We have been more inclined to act where our interests and values are both at stake and where our resources can affect tangible improvement, as in Bosnia and Kosovo. In each of these instances, atrocities against, and the expulsion of, people in the heart of Europe undermined the very values over which we had fought two World Wars and the Cold War. Left unchecked, they could have spread elsewhere throughout Europe and harmed the NATO alliance. We thus saw that our interests and values were affected to a sufficient degree to warrant U.S. military intervention in both Bosnia and Kosovo.

As we look to the future, our strategy must therefore be sufficiently robust so that when we choose to engage, we can do so to prevent conflict, assist failing states, or counter potential regional aggressors as necessary.

Preparing for an Uncertain Future

Meeting this widening array of new threats to our security will require us to transform our capabilities and organizations. Within our military, this transformation has taken several forms: focused science and technology efforts; concept development and experimentation by the Services, combatant commands, and the Joint Staff; robust processes to implement change; and new approaches to foster a culture of bold innovation and dynamic leadership.

The process of transformation must not end solely with defense. Preparation must also include diplomatic, intelligence, law enforcement, and economic efforts if we are to meet the new threats that rapidity of technological change brings to the hands of adversaries, potential and actual. Our government is therefore implementing interagency approaches to formulate, and then execute, policy and plans for dealing with potential contingencies. In addition, preventative diplomacy, often undergirded by the deterrence of our full military capabilities, may help contain or resolve problems before they erupt into crises or contingency operations.

Summary

The elements of engagement -- adapting alliances; encouraging the reorientation of other states, including former adversaries; encouraging democratization, open markets, free trade, and sustainable development; preventing conflict; countering potential regional aggressors; confronting new threats; and steering international peace and stability operations -- define the Nation's blueprint for a strategy of engagement. These elements support three strategic concepts for engagement: shaping the international environment, responding to threats and crises, and preparing for an uncertain future. The blueprint and the concepts it supports have served the United States well in a rapidly changing world. Refined by experience, the strategy is a wise roadmap for national security in the 21st century.

Guiding Principles of Engagement

Both our goals, and the policies we pursue to achieve these goals, must reflect two guiding principles that influence both our national character and legacy: ***protecting our national interests*** and ***advancing our values.*** Throughout history, all sovereign nations have been guided by protection of their national interests, even if they have defined these interests quite differently. Many countries have also been guided by a desire to advance their values. Few, however, have chosen to advance those values principally through the power of their example instead of the might of their military. Historically, the United States has chosen to let our example be the strongest voice of our values. Both our goals and the policies we pursue to achieve these goals reflect these guiding principles.

Protecting our National Interests

Our national interests are wide-ranging. They cover those requirements essential to the survival and well being of our Nation as well as the desire to see us, and others, abide by principles such as the rule of law, upon which our republic was founded.

We divide our national interests into three categories: vital, important, and humanitarian. Vital interests are those directly connected to the survival, safety, and vitality of our nation. Among these are the physical security of our territory and that of our allies, the safety of our citizens both at home and abroad, protection against WMD proliferation, the economic well-being of our society, and the protection of our critical infrastructures--including energy, banking and finance, telecommunications, transportation, water systems, vital human services, and government services--from disruption intended to cripple their operation. We will do what we must to defend these interests. This may involve the use of military force, including unilateral action, where deemed necessary or appropriate.

The second category, important national interests, affects our national well being or that of the world in which we live. Principally, this may include developments in regions where America holds a significant economic or political stake, issues with significant global environmental impact, infrastructure disruptions that destabilize but do not cripple smooth economic activity, and crises that could cause destabilizing economic turmoil or humanitarian movement. Examples of when we have acted to protect important national interests include our successful efforts to end the brutal conflict and restore peace in Kosovo, or our assistance to our Asian and Pacific allies and friends in support of the restoration of order and transition to nationhood in East Timor.

The third category is humanitarian and other longer-term interests. Examples include reacting to natural and manmade disasters; acting to halt gross violations of human rights; supporting emerging democracies; encouraging adherence to the rule of law and civilian control of the military; conducting Joint Recovery Operations worldwide to account for our country's war dead; promoting sustainable development and environmental protection; or facilitating humanitarian demining.

Threats or challenges to our national interests could require a range of responses. Wherever possible, we seek to avert conflict or relieve humanitarian disasters through diplomacy and cooperation with a wide range of partners, including other governments, international institutions, and non-governmental organizations. Prevention of crises, through the proactive use of such diplomatic, economic, political and military presence tools, will not only save lives but also will prevent a much greater drain of fiscal resources than its alternative -- managing conflict.

Advancing American Values

The protection of national interests is not the sole factor behind the various expressions of U.S. national resolve. Since the beginning of our democracy, our policies and actions have also been guided by our core values -- political and economic freedom, respect for human rights, and the rule of law. In keeping with these values, we have lent our encouragement, support, and assistance to those nations and peoples that freely desire to achieve those same blessings of liberty. Pursuing policies that are guided by these values, and the open economic and political processes through which they are typically manifested, will in the long term strengthen international peace and stability, and reinforce the positive aspects of globalization.

Where Interests Meet Values

There are times when the nexus of our interests and values exists in a compelling combination that demands action -- diplomatic, economic, or military. At times throughout our history, our survival as a nation has been at stake and military action was the only possible recourse. On other occasions, our survival as a nation has not been at stake but our national interests have nonetheless been challenged. When such challenges to our interests occur in concert with morally compelling challenges to our values, the American people expect their government to take action. During the course of this Administration, we have employed military force only in circumstances in which our national interests were at stake and our values were challenged.

Preserving our interests and values has never been without cost, and every generation has been asked to bear a portion of the price of freedom. From a bridge at Concord over two centuries ago to the air over Kosovo last year, on numerous occasions Americans have been called upon to stand up for their interests, interests which are often inextricably linked with their values.

Today, 250,000 U.S. forces are stationed or deployed overseas to protect and advance our nation's interests and values -- down from a Cold War peak of 500,000. Of this, we maintain a continuous overseas presence of over 200,000 in places like Germany, Japan, and South Korea, while about 30,000 are currently involved in operations. These include nearly 20,000 stationed around the Persian Gulf to contain Iraq, roughly 10,000 in Bosnia and Kosovo, and 1,000 in the Sinai. Other forces, such as those rotationally deployed to the Mediterranean, the Pacific Ocean and the Arabian Gulf, remain involved in routine operations. Our diplomatic corps -- the Civil and Foreign Services -- also bear an important part of protecting and advancing our interests, often in the furthest reaches of the globe, through embassies, consulates, and missions worldwide.

The Efficacy of Engagement

Our strategy of engagement has allowed us to accrue a range of benefits, including sustained, relative peace, expanded trade and investment opportunities brought by globalization, and a large increase in the number of states that share our democratic values. We have exercised strong leadership in the international community to shape the international security environment in ways that promote peace, stability, prosperity, and democratic governance. We have transformed our alliances and reinvigorated relationships with friends and partners; forged broad relationships with former adversaries; fostered new relations with transitional states; and deterred major hostilities.

Enhancing Our Security at Home and Abroad

There are clear indicators that engagement is achieving our national security goals in this rapidly changing world. First, engagement has produced many benefits that enhance our security at home and abroad. The overseas presence of our military forces helps deter or even prevent conflict. It assures our allies of our support and displays our resolve to potential enemies. It allows for maximum military cooperation with our allies and therefore encourages burdensharing. Forward-deployed forces permit us to identify emerging security problems, and then facilitate a swift response, if necessary. Ongoing operations in Southwest Asia and Southeastern Europe have improved the current security environment by ensuring that a return to peace is sustained. Our new embassies in the countries of the former Soviet Union, and in some 140 other countries, allow the U.S. to advance America's interests and values in real time, and to immediately detect opportunities and challenges to these interests. Other aspects of our engagement policies, such as non-proliferation programs like the Expanded Threat Reduction Initiative (ETRI), have, within the framework of START 1, stabilized the security environment. Over 5,000 nuclear warheads, 600 missile launchers, 540 land-based and submarine launched inter-continental ballistic missiles, 64 heavy bombers, and 15 missile submarines have been deactivated and potential proliferation of WMD or their delivery means averted. These efforts have made the world a much safer place.

We have also seen international engagement enhance our ability to address asymmetric threats to our security, such as acts of terrorism and the desired procurement and use of WMD by potential regional aggressors. International counterterrorism cooperation, for example, led to the pre-emptive arrest of individuals planning to terrorize Americans at home and abroad celebrating the Millennium. Engagement efforts have already assembled an impressive record of international cooperation to harmonize legislation on terrorist offenses, conduct research and development, and create databases on terrorism. Strong U.S. overseas presence and engagement, enhanced by a network of multilateral agreements and arrangements, has enabled us to contain the proliferation of nuclear, biological, and chemical weapons and their means of delivery by potential regional aggressors. Inspections done at point of origin for goods destined for the U.S. improves our nonproliferation and border security efforts and even enhances cargo throughput. In other cases, it has actually interrupted the flow of sensitive goods to those countries. Robust engagement in support of law enforcement efforts of partner nations has resulted in the dismantling of a number of major drug trafficking organizations and the interdiction of significant quantities of elicit [sic] drugs that would otherwise have reached U.S. or other consumer markets. Together, efforts that focus on asymmetric threats to our security will reduce our potential vulnerability despite an increasingly inter-connected world.

Economic Benefits that Promote Prosperity

Engagement has had clear economic benefits that promote prosperity around the globe. This strategy provides stability to the world economic system on which the U.S. economy depends. Our involvement in international economic organizations like the G-8, G-20, World Trade Organization (WTO) and Organization for Economic Cooperation and Development (OECD) has helped build stable, resilient global economic and financial systems that promote strong, global prosperity. The U.S. - China Bilateral WTO agreement, for example, will reduce China's tariffs on U.S. priority agricultural products from an average of 31% to 14%. It will reduce similar tariffs on U.S. industrial products from 24.6% to 9.4%. Such agreements expand U.S. market access and bring new goods and services to these markets at lower cost. Overall, the Administration has concluded 304 trade agreements, and created a series of new fora for economic dialogue, that now include the Asia Pacific Economic Cooperation (APEC) forum, the Transatlantic Economic Partnership, and the ongoing development work on the Free Trade Area of the Americas (FTAA). This has led to numerous economic and financial agreements/reforms in international institutions that bring stability to the global marketplace that is so essential for America's economic health and economic security. As a result, total U.S. exports of goods and services have grown by over 75% since 1992. Measures to strengthen the architecture of the international financial system, including through increased transparency and reform of the International Monetary Fund (IMF) and World Bank, have helped put the international economy on a sound footing after recent financial crises and build a stronger global financial system. In addition, WTO agreements to strengthen and expand trade in information technology goods, financial services, basic telecommunications services, and electronic commerce have secured open markets in sectors key to American economic vitality, and laid the groundwork for future liberalization in agriculture, services, and other areas.

Military presence and engagement activities can also provide similar economic stability. Our naval presence ensures that international waters, the sea lines of communication, and ports remain open to commercial shipping, and our ground, air, and naval forces in Southwest Asia deter threats to the free flow of Middle East oil. The clearest and longest standing example of what overseas presence can do for economic stability is found in the sizeable U.S. military force found on the Korean peninsula since 1953. Currently 37,000 strong, U.S. forces have helped the South Koreans rebuild and grow, and now both sides support the continued presence of U.S. forces as a measure of stability. U.S. actions that protect the free flow of natural resources and finished goods provide an environment for sustained economic productivity. Engagement, through military, diplomatic, or other governmental entities, also enables rapid response to computer network incidents and attacks that harm our economy. International government-to-government cooperation, for example, led to the law enforcement action that definitively determined the source of some of the distributed, denial of service attacks in February 2000.

Promoting Democracy and Human Rights

Finally, engagement has had political and diplomatic benefits that promote democracy and human rights. Our policies bring our country's strengths directly to international publics, governments, and militaries, with the hope that this exposure may inspire others to promote democracy and the free market. Whether we're advising foreign governments on the conduct of free elections, teaching foreign troops about the importance of civilian control of the military, aiding international relief agencies in the wake of natural disasters, or in the diplomatic day-to-day efforts of our diplomats in 273 missions around the world, an engaged America brings its values to the world's doorstep. For example, the multi-faceted program for engagement in Africa is having a clear impact on the cultivation of democracy on the continent. From Kampala to Cape Town, from Dakar to Dar-es-Salaam, Africans have new hopes for democracy, peace, and prosperity. Although many challenges yet remain, visible change is occurring. Through our diplomatic missions, over 20 nations across Africa have requested and are receiving assistance to develop judiciary, legal, media, and civil society systems to build necessary institutions to sustain democratic ideals. We are assisting democratic transitions in Nigeria and South Africa.

In our own hemisphere, our engagement efforts have promoted free and fair elections throughout the hemisphere. In Southeast Europe, the Dayton Accords have sustained the peace in Bosnia, permitted a civil society with opposition parties and non-governmental organizations to take root, begun reforms of police and court systems, and allowed national and local elections to take place. The transformation is not complete and progress is not irreversible, but it is unmistakable. The best role model is a visible one.

In summary, a strategy of engagement reaps significant benefits for our Nation -- benefits that actively support our goals of security, prosperity and democracy, yet always remain in consonance with our principles of protecting our national interests and advancing our values. Indeed, there is no other viable policy choice in this global era.

II. Implementing the Strategy

Into the 21st century, the United States must continue to adapt to changes brought by globalization such that we foster close cooperative relations with the world's most influential nations while preserving our ability to shape those nations capable of having an adverse effect upon our well-being and way of life. A stable, peaceful international security environment is the desired endstate -- one in which our nation, citizens and interests are not threatened. It is important that we work to enhance the health and safety of our citizens by promoting a cleaner global environment and effective strategies to combat infectious disease. We must work to ensure that the United States continues to prosper through increasingly open international markets and sustainable growth in the global economy, and that democratic values, respect for human rights, and the rule of law are increasingly accepted.

Chapter II describes how we intend to utilize the instruments at our disposal to implement our strategy for engagement and, in the process, achieve the goals of security, prosperity, and democracy -- our vision for ourselves and others in the 21st century.

Enhancing Security at Home and Abroad

Our strategy for enhancing U.S. security has three principal elements: shaping the international security environment, responding to threats and crises, and preparing for an uncertain future.

Shaping the International Environment

The United States seeks to shape the international environment through a variety of means, including diplomacy, economic cooperation, international assistance, arms control and nonproliferation efforts, military presence and engagement activities, and global health initiatives. These activities enhance U.S. security by promoting regional security; enhancing economic progress; supporting military activities abroad, international law enforcement cooperation, and environmental efforts; and preventing, reducing or deterring the diverse threats we face today. These measures adapt and strengthen alliances and friendships, maintain U.S. influence in key regions, and encourage adherence to international norms.

The U.S. intelligence community provides various Federal agencies with critical support for the full range of our involvement abroad. Comprehensive collection and analytic capabilities are needed to provide warning of threats to U.S. national security, give analytical support to the policy, law enforcement, and military communities, enable near-real time intelligence while retaining global perspective, identify opportunities for advancing our national interests, and maintain our information advantage in the international arena. We place the highest priority on monitoring the most serious threats to U.S. security. These include countries or other entities potentially hostile to the United States; proliferation of nuclear, biological, and chemical weapons and their means of delivery; other transnational threats, including terrorism, drug trafficking, proliferation of small arms and light weapons, other international crime, and potential threats to our critical infrastructure such as computer network attack; potential regional conflicts that might affect U.S. national security interests; illegal economic or uncontrolled refugee migration; and threats to U.S. forces and citizens abroad.

Diplomacy

Active diplomacy is critical to advancing our national security. The work of our missions and representatives around the world serves a number of shaping functions. Examples include adapting alliances, as the State and Defense Departments do when they work to ensure that NATO "candidate" militaries will be interoperable with those of current NATO members; deterring aggression, mediating disputes, and resolving conflicts as shown by our efforts to dampen the momentum to conflict in South Asia and the Middle East; promoting the trade and investment opportunities that increase U.S. economic prosperity; and confronting new threats.

While crisis management is an important foreign policy function, crisis prevention is far preferable. Throughout the 1990s, the United States has most frequently chosen a policy of preventive diplomacy to avert conflict as well as humanitarian and other emergencies. Bringing disputing parties to the table is less costly in lives and resources than separating warring parties; helping failing states is less burdensome than rebuilding failed states; and feeding the hungry is far more effective and easier than treating victims of diseases wrought by malnutrition.

Our diplomatic efforts are often multilateral. Consistent with our global leadership role, it is incumbent upon the United States to maintain its financial and political support for international institutions such as the United Nations, the International Monetary Fund, the World Bank, and the World Trade Organization. We must continue to work to ensure we meet our financial obligations to international organizations.

Likewise, domestically, we must remain committed to supporting the State Department, the U.S. Agency for International Development, the Peace Corps, and other vehicles of U.S. diplomacy. Our diplomatic infrastructure must be updated to meet critical productivity and information age requirements to effectively serve our diplomatic and consular efforts worldwide. Modernization of embassies, consulates, and our diplomatic telecommunications and information infrastructure is essential to advancing and protecting vital national interests overseas. Our embassies and consulates host critical elements of peacetime power: diplomatic personnel, commercial, defense, and legal attaches, and consular and security officers dedicated to protecting Americans at home and abroad. Our commitment in properly resourcing these modernization plans is essential if we are to have the future diplomatic infrastructure capable of supporting and enhancing our leadership role worldwide.

Such enhancements to our diplomatic infrastructure will also help attract a new generation of professionals whose skill, dedication, and creativity are at the heart of our ability to use diplomacy to protect American interests. To both attract and retain these individuals, we must take every measure to keep our personnel safe overseas. The State Department is therefore implementing a broad program of security enhancements in response to continued threats of terrorism directed at U.S. diplomatic and consular facilities overseas. The investment is warranted. The cost to sustain and protect the diplomatic components of our peacetime power is a tiny fraction of the price associated with the crises averted by their presence.

Public Diplomacy

We have an obligation and opportunity to harness the tools of public diplomacy to advance U.S. leadership around the world by engaging international publics on U.S. principles and policies. The global advance of individual freedom and information technologies like the Internet has increased the ability of citizens and organizations to influence the policies of governments to an unprecedented extent. This makes our public diplomacy -- efforts to transmit information and messages to peoples around the world -- an increasingly vital component of our national security strategy. Our programs enhance our nation's ability to inform and influence foreign publics in support of our national interests, and broaden the dialogue between U.S. citizens and institutions and their counterparts abroad. Some even improve mutual understanding by reaching out to future leaders and inform the opinions of current leaders through academic, professional, and cultural exchanges. Successful diplomatic relations between the United States and other countries depend upon establishing trust and creating credible partnerships based on this trust.

Effective use of our nation's information capabilities to counter misinformation and incitement, mitigate inter-ethnic conflict, promote independent media organizations and the free flow of information, and support democratic participation helps advance U.S. interests abroad. International Public Information activities, as defined by Presidential Decision Directive 68 (PDD-68), are designed to improve our capability to coordinate independent public diplomacy, public affairs and other national security information-related efforts to ensure they are more successfully integrated into foreign and national security policy making and execution.

International Assistance

The United States has a history of providing generous foreign assistance in an effort to promote global stability. From the Marshall Plan to the present, our foreign assistance has expanded free markets, promoted democracy and human rights, contained major health threats, encouraged sustainable global population growth, promoted environmental protection, and defused humanitarian crises.

Expanding debt relief is a key element of our international assistance agenda. In 1999, the G-8 agreed to a reduction in bilateral debt between member countries and Heavily Indebted Poor Countries (HIPC). This effort encourages international financial institutions to link debt reduction to other efforts to alleviate poverty, promote economic development, and thereby create stronger partners around the world for trade and investment, security, and democracy. To show our commitment to this agreement we have stood firmly behind efforts to provide 100% debt relief in countries where the funds being used to service bilateral debt will finance the basic human needs of a population.

The United States intends that these nations not be left behind, instead joining in the positive economic prosperity made possible through participation in the international economic community. Our role in the World Bank and other multilateral development banks supports mutual goals to provide developing countries with the financial and technical assistance necessary to assimilate them into the global economy. Such efforts lift peoples out of poverty, and typically result in substantial growth of U.S. exports to the aided countries.

Finally, our philanthropic history is such that we routinely act to mitigate human suffering in the wake of both natural and man-made disasters. From the U.S. Agency for International Development's disaster assistance and food aid, to the State Department's refugee assistance, to grants to non-governmental relief organizations, to the Defense Department's Humanitarian Assistance Program, the United States has found multiple avenues to relieve the suffering of disaster victims worldwide with coordinated targeted relief efforts.

Arms Control and Nonproliferation

Arms control and nonproliferation initiatives are an essential element of our national security strategy of enhancing security at home and abroad. They closely complement and strengthen our efforts to defend our nation through our own military strength while seeking to make the world a less dangerous place. We pursue verifiable arms control and nonproliferation agreements that support our efforts to prevent the spread and use of NBC weapons, materials, expertise, and means of delivery; halt the use of conventional weapons that cause unnecessary suffering; and contribute to regional stability at lower levels of armaments. In addition, by increasing transparency in the size, structure and operations of military forces and building confidence in the intentions of other countries, arms control agreements and confidence-building measures constrain inventories of dangerous weapons, reduce incentives and opportunities to initiate an attack, reduce the mutual suspicions that arise from and spur on armaments competition, and help provide the assurance of security necessary to strengthen cooperative relationships and direct resources to safer, more productive endeavors.

Verifiable reductions in strategic offensive arms and the steady shift toward less destabilizing systems remain essential to our strategy. The START I Treaty's entry into force in December 1994 charted the course for reductions in the deployed strategic nuclear forces of the United States and the former Soviet Union. The other countries of the former Soviet Union, besides Russia, that had nuclear weapons on their soil -- Belarus, Kazakhstan and Ukraine -- have become non-nuclear weapons states under the Nuclear Nonproliferation Treaty (NPT). If the START II Treaty enters into force, the United States and Russia will each be limited to 3,000 to 3,500 strategic nuclear weapons. START II also will prohibit land-based missiles from being deployed with more than one warhead and eliminate heavy land-based missiles entirely. On September 26, 1997, the United States and Russia signed a START II Protocol extending the end date for reductions to 2007, and exchanged letters on early deactivation by 2003 of those strategic nuclear delivery systems to be eliminated by 2007. The Senate approved the ratification of START II in January 1996; the Duma ratified the START II Treaty and the 1997 START II Protocol in April 2000.

At the Helsinki Summit in March 1997, Presidents Clinton and Yeltsin agreed to START III guidelines that, if adopted, will cap the number of strategic nuclear warheads deployed in each country at 2,000 - 2,500 by the end of 2007 -- reducing both our arsenals by 80% from Cold War heights. They also agreed that, in order to promote the irreversibility of deep reductions, a START III agreement will include measures relating to the transparency of strategic nuclear warhead inventories and the destruction of strategic nuclear warheads. In addition, the Presidents agreed to explore possible confidence-building and transparency measures relating to nuclear long-range, sea-launched cruise missiles and tactical nuclear systems.

The Anti-Ballistic Missile (ABM) Treaty remains a cornerstone of strategic stability, and the United States is committed to continue efforts to enhance the Treaty's viability and effectiveness. On September 26, 1997, representatives of the United States, Russia, Belarus, Kazakhstan and Ukraine signed or initialed five agreements relating to the ABM Treaty. At the Cologne G-8 Summit in June 1999, Presidents Clinton and Yeltsin reiterated their determination to achieve earliest possible ratification and entry into force of those agreements. The two presidents also reaffirmed at Cologne their existing obligations under Article XIII of the ABM Treaty to consider possible changes in the strategic situation that have a bearing on the ABM Treaty and, as appropriate, possible proposals for further increasing the viability of the Treaty. They also agreed to begin discussions on the ABM Treaty in parallel with discussions on START III. The United States has proposed that the ABM Treaty be modified to accommodate possible deployment of a limited National Missile Defense (NMD) system that would counter new threats by states that threaten international peace and security while preserving strategic stability.

At the June 4, 2000, Moscow summit, Presidents Clinton and Putin signed a Joint Statement of Principles on Strategic Stability. The Principles state that the international community faces a dangerous and growing threat of proliferation of weapons of mass destruction and their means of delivery, including missiles and missile technologies, and that there is a need to address these threats. The Principles recalled the existing provisions of the ABM Treaty, to consider changes in the strategic situation that have a bearing on the provisions of the treaty, and, as appropriate, to consider possible proposals for further increasing the viability of the Treaty. The Principles also record agreement to intensify discussions on both ABM issues and START III.

The United States has also made clear to Russia that we are prepared to engage in serious cooperation to address the emerging ballistic missile threat, and we have identified a number of specific ideas for discussion. At the same June 4, 2000, Moscow Summit, Presidents Clinton and Putin signed an agreement to establish a Joint Center for exchanging early warning data on ballistic missile launches. The agreement will significantly reduce the danger that ballistic missiles could be launched inadvertently on false warning of attack. It will also promote increased mutual confidence in the capabilities of the ballistic missile early warning systems of both sides. The Presidents also agreed to explore more far-reaching cooperation to address missile threats.

On July 21, 2000, in Okinawa, Presidents Clinton and Putin issued a Joint Statement on Cooperation on Strategic Stability, which identifies specific areas and projects for cooperation to control the spread of missiles, missile technology, and weapons of mass destruction. On September 6, 2000, in New York, Presidents Clinton and Putin signed a Joint Statement on the Strategic Stability Cooperation Initiative and Implementation Plan, which provides further detail and an agreed timetable for pursuing cooperation in these areas, including the establishment of a ballistic missile and space launch vehicle pre-launch notification regime in which other states would be invited to participate. Most recently, the United States and Russia signed a bilateral pre-launch notification agreement on December 16, 2000.

To be secure, we must not only have a strong military; we must also take the lead in building a safer, more responsible world. We have a fundamental responsibility to limit the spread of nuclear weapons and reduce the danger of nuclear war. To this end, the United States remains committed to bringing the Comprehensive Nuclear Test Ban Treaty (CTBT) into force.

To date, 160 countries have signed -- and 68 have ratified -- the Treaty prohibiting all nuclear explosions. The 68 include 31 of the 44 countries named in the Treaty whose ratification is necessary for entry into force. The CTBT will, in effect, constrain nuclear weapons development. The United States ended nuclear testing eight years ago; upon entry into force, the CTBT will require other state entities to also refrain from testing. We are confident in the safety and reliability of the U.S. nuclear stockpile, and we are confident that a fully supported and sustained stockpile stewardship program will enable us to continue to maintain America's nuclear deterrent capability. However, if we find we cannot, we would have the option of using our supreme national interest withdrawal rights under the Treaty in order to conduct whatever nuclear testing is necessary.

The CTBT will put in place a worldwide network of sensors for detecting nuclear explosions. With over 300 stations around the globe -- including 31 in Russia, 11 in China, and 17 in the Middle East -- this international monitoring system will improve our ability to monitor nuclear explosions and catch cheaters. The United States already has dozens of monitoring stations of its own; the CTBT will allow us to take advantage of other countries' stations, while also creating new ones. The Treaty also will give us the right to request on-site inspections of sites in other countries where nuclear tests are suspected to have taken place.

As a matter of policy, the United States will maintain its moratorium on nuclear testing, pending entry into force of the CTBT, and we are encouraging all other states to do the same. We are also encouraging all states that have not signed and ratified the CTBT to do so. Despite the unfortunate rejection of the CTBT by the U.S. Senate, we remain committed to obtaining Senate advice and consent for ratification of this treaty. United States ratification will encourage other states to ratify, enable the United States to lead the international effort to gain CTBT entry into force, and strengthen international norms against nuclear testing. Simply stated, the United States must be prepared to lead by example.

The NPT, the cornerstone of international nuclear nonproliferation regime, reinforces regional and global security by creating and sustaining confidence in the non-nuclear commitments of its parties. It was an indispensable precondition for the denuclearization of Ukraine, Kazakhstan, Belarus and South Africa. We seek to ensure that the NPT remains a strong and vital element of global security by achieving universal adherence and full compliance by its parties with their Treaty obligations. A Review Conference held in May 2000, the first in fifteen years with a consensus document, strengthened the global nuclear nonproliferation norm and demonstrated that support for this critical Treaty is broad and deep. We won our case by vigorously promoting the value of the NPT in preventing the spread of nuclear weapons while continuing policies designed to reduce U.S. reliance on nuclear weapons and to work for their ultimate elimination.

The safeguards system of the International Atomic Energy Agency (IAEA) is an essential component of the nuclear nonproliferation regime. We seek widespread adoption of the IAEA's strengthened safeguards system and to ensure that the IAEA has the resources necessary to fulfill its obligations. We are working to amend the Convention on the Physical Protection of Nuclear Material to ensure that its standards cover national activities as well as international transfers of nuclear material, which complements our effort to enhance IAEA safeguards. We also seek the immediate commencement of negotiations to achieve a Fissile Material Cutoff Treaty at the Geneva Conference on Disarmament. Halting production of fissile materials for nuclear explosions would cap the supply of nuclear materials available worldwide for weapons, a key step in halting the spread of nuclear weapons. A coordinated effort by the intelligence community and law enforcement agencies to detect, prevent, and deter illegal trafficking in fissile materials is essential to our counterproliferation efforts. So is the Material Protection, Control and Accounting program, which enhances security for former Soviet nuclear materials and helps prevent them from ending up in the hands of terrorists or proliferant states. We also recognize that nuclear weapon free zone treaties and protocols that conform with long-standing U.S. criteria can also advance nuclear nonproliferation goals.

Through the Nunn-Lugar Cooperative Threat Reduction (CTR) Program and other initiatives, we aim to strengthen controls over weapons-usable fissile material and prevent the theft or diversion of NBC weapons and related material and technology from the former Soviet Union. The CTR Program has effectively supported enhanced safety, security, accounting, and centralized control measures for nuclear weapons and fissile materials in the former Soviet Union. It has assisted Ukraine, Kazakhstan and Belarus in becoming non-nuclear weapons states and will continue to assist Russia in meeting its START obligations. The CTR Program is also supporting measures to eliminate and prevent the proliferation of chemical weapons and biological weapon-related capabilities, and it has supported many ongoing military reductions and reform measures in the former Soviet Union.

The Nonproliferation and Disarmament Fund (NDF) is a sharply focused fund to permit rapid response to unanticipated, high priority requirements or opportunities to: 1) halt the spread of WMD, their delivery systems, and related technology; 2) limit the spread of advanced conventional weapons and related technology; and 3) eliminate existing weapons. NDF activities in Central Europe and the NIS have included the elimination of SCUD and SS-23 missiles, the procurement of HEU, the development and deployment of automated systems to license and track sensitive technologies, and the acquisition of nuclear material detection equipment.

In 1999, the President launched the Expanded Threat Reduction Initiative (ETRI). This effort is designed to address the new security challenges in Russia and the other Newly Independent States (NIS) caused by that year's financial crisis, including preventing the proliferation of NBC weapons, reducing the threat posed by residual NBC weapons, and stabilizing the military. This initiative builds on the success of existing programs, such as the CTR program, the Material Protection, Control and Accounting program, and the Science Centers. A new component of our nuclear security program will greatly enhance the security of fissile material by concentrating it at fewer, well-protected sites, and new programs will increase the security of facilities and experts formerly associated with the Soviet Union's biological weapons effort.

At the June 4, 2000, Clinton-Putin summit, the United States and Russia reached agreement on the management and disposition of plutonium designated as no longer required for defense purposes. The agreement entered into force after Prime Minister Kasyanov and Vice President Gore signed it on September 1, 2000. Under the agreement, each government commits to irreversibly transform 34 metric tons of excess weapon-grade plutonium to a form that will be unusable for weapons. The agreement establishes the goals, timelines, and conditions for ensuring that this plutonium can never again be used for weapons or any other military purposes.

Implementation of the Plutonium Management and Disposition Agreement is contingent on sufficient international assistance for the Russian program. At the Okinawa G-8 Summit in July 2000, leaders took an additional step to this end. The final communiqué stated that their goal for the next summit is to develop an international financing plan for plutonium management and disposition based on a detailed project plan, and a multilateral framework to coordinate this cooperation. They also committed to expand cooperation to other interested countries beyond the G-8 in order to gain the widest possible international support, and to explore the potential for both public and private funding.

Over the past year, the United States Government provided leadership for the multilateral cooperation effort, particularly in the context of an informal G-8 working group, which coordinated with the G-8 Nonproliferation Experts Group. (NPEG). Preparations for the Genoa summit will be under the auspices of a formally established Plutonium Disposition Planning Group to be co-chaired by the United States and the Russian Federation. We are purchasing tons of highly enriched uranium from dismantled Russian nuclear weapons for conversion into commercial reactor fuel. We are helping redirect dozens of former Soviet NBC facilities and tens of thousands of former NBC scientists in Eurasia from military activities to beneficial civilian research.

In support of U.S. efforts to prevent proliferation of NBC expertise and materials in the NIS, Eastern Europe, and across borders, the Departments of Defense, Energy, and Commerce, the U.S. Customs Service, and the FBI are engaging in programs that assist governments in developing effective export control systems and in developing capabilities to prevent, deter, or detect such proliferation. These programs provide training, equipment, advice, and services to law enforcement and border security agencies in these countries.

We seek to strengthen the Biological Weapons Convention (BWC) with a new international regime to enhance compliance. We are also working hard to implement and enforce the Chemical Weapons Convention (CWC). The United States Congress underscored the importance of these efforts in October 1998 by passing implementing legislation. In late 1999, the Executive Order (EO 13128), Presidential Decision Directive (PDD-70), and two new regulations were completed, enabling the United States to submit commercial declarations and commence commercial facility inspections in the middle of 2000.

The Administration also seeks to prevent destabilizing buildups of conventional arms and to limit access to sensitive technical information, equipment, and technologies by strengthening international regimes, including the Wassenaar Arrangement on Export Controls for Conventional Arms and Dual-Use Goods and Technologies, the Australia Group (for chemical and biological weapons), the Missile Technology Control Regime, the Nuclear Suppliers Group (NSG), and the Zangger Committee (NSG and Zangger ensure that IAEA safeguards are applied to nuclear exports). At the NATO 50th Anniversary Summit, Allied leaders agreed to enhance NATO's ability to deal both politically and militarily with the proliferation of WMD and the means of their delivery. To this end, we have worked with our Alliance partners to establish the NATO WMD Center and to promote invigorated discussions of nonproliferation issues in the NATO Senior Political Military and Defense Groups on Proliferation.

Regional nonproliferation efforts are particularly important in three critical proliferation zones: the Korean Peninsula, Southwest Asia, and South Asia. On the Korean Peninsula, we are implementing the 1994 Agreed Framework, which requires full compliance by North Korea to live up to its nuclear nonproliferation obligations. We also seek to convince North Korea to halt its indigenous missile program and exports of missile systems and technologies; something emphasized during a November 2000 visit to Pyongyang by the Secretary of State. In the Middle East and Southwest Asia, we encourage regional confidence-building measures and arms control agreements that address the legitimate security concerns of all parties. We continue efforts to thwart and roll back both Iran's development of NBC weapons and long-range missiles, and also Iraq's efforts to reconstitute its NBC programs. In South Asia, we seek to persuade India and Pakistan to refrain from weaponizing or deploying nuclear weapons, testing or deploying missiles capable of delivering nuclear weapons, and further producing fissile material for nuclear weapons. We also urge India and Pakistan to adhere fully to international nonproliferation standards and to sign and ratify the CTBT.

Over the past three years, the United States has worked to ensure that the landmark 1990 Conventional Armed Forces in Europe (CFE) Treaty remains a cornerstone of European peace, security and stability into the 21st century. On November 19, 1999, we joined the other 29 CFE States Parties in signing an Adaptation Agreement that eliminates obsolete bloc-to-bloc limits and replaces them with a system of national and territorial ceilings. It will also enhance transparency through more information and inspections, strengthen requirements for host nation consent to the presence of foreign forces, and open the treaty to accession by other European nations. The accompanying CFE Final Act reflects a number of important political commitments, including agreements on the complete withdrawal of Russian armed forces from Moldova and partial withdrawal of Russian forces from Georgia.

The United States is a world leader in the effort to curb the harmful proliferation and destabilizing accumulation of small arms and light weapons (SA/LW) such as automatic rifles, machine guns, rocket-propelled grenades, light mortars and man-portable anti-aircraft missiles. Inexpensive, widely available, and easy to use, these weapons exacerbate regional conflicts, expand casualties, increase crime, and hinder economic development. They can jeopardize the safety of peacekeepers, potentially putting U.S. Forces at risk.

To reduce this threat, the United States is urging countries to adopt effective export controls, brokering regulations, permanent marking, anti-smuggling measures, and embargo enforcement. Global efforts focus on securing a Firearms Protocol to the UN Transnational Organized Crime Convention and seeking international agreement through the UN 2001 Conference on Illicit Trafficking in SA/LW. The United States also works with regional partners in the OSCE, NATO/EAPC, OAS, OAU, the ASEAN Regional Forum, and elsewhere. The United States provides some technical assistance to countries trying to prevent SA/LW trafficking and actively supports efforts to destroy excess stocks of SA/LW worldwide, often partnering with like-minded countries such as Norway.

The United States is also committed to ending the threat to innocent civilians from anti-personnel landmines (APLs). We have already taken major steps toward this goal while ensuring our ability to meet international obligations and provide for the safety and security of our men and women in uniform. President Clinton has directed the Defense Department to end the use of all APLs, including self-destructing APLs, outside Korea by 2003 and to pursue aggressively the objective of having APL alternatives ready for Korea by 2006. We are also aggressively pursuing alternatives to our mixed anti-tank systems that contain anti-personnel submunitions. We have made clear that the United States will sign the Ottawa Convention by 2006 if by then we have succeeded in identifying and fielding suitable alternatives to our self-destructing APLs and mixed anti-tank systems.

In May 1999, we gained Senate advice and consent to ratification of the Amended Mines Protocol to the Convention on Conventional Weapons. This agreement addresses the worldwide humanitarian problem caused by APLs by banning the use of non-detectable APLs and severely limiting the use of long-duration APLs to clearly marked and monitored fields that effectively keep out civilians. We have established a permanent ban on APL exports and are seeking to universalize an export ban through the Conference on Disarmament in Geneva. We are supporting humanitarian demining programs worldwide through engagement with mine-afflicted nations and the international community. We have taken a lead role in establishing the International Test and Evaluation Program, through which nations will develop agreed standards and test procedures for various pieces of demining equipment and will then test against those standards. To date, the United States has provided over $400 million through the

U.S. Humanitarian Demining Program. The Demining 2010 Initiative, which is independent of the Humanitarian Demining Program, advocates increased efforts in the United States and abroad and develops public-private partnerships to support these programs.

The effectiveness of the panoply of arms control agreements described above, as well as that of our nonproliferation activities, rests on maintaining and enhancing our monitoring capabilities. We must keep ahead of potential attempts by others at denial and deception. To do so, we must maintain current monitoring assets and have a vigorous research and development program that will translate new technologies into enhanced capabilities. These efforts will increase our confidence in the viability of existing agreements and enable us to conclude new ones to further decrease the risks of armed conflicts.

Military Activities

The U.S. military is a very visible and critical pillar of our effort to shape the international security environment in ways that protect and promote U.S. interests. It is not, however, a substitute for other forms of engagement, such as diplomatic, economic, scientific, technological, cultural, and educational activities. We must always be mindful that the primary mission of our Armed Forces is to deter and, if necessary, to fight and win conflicts in which our vital interests are threatened. Through overseas presence and peacetime engagement activities, such as defense cooperation, security assistance, regional centers for security studies, training, and exercises with allies and friends, our Armed Forces help to deter aggression and coercion, build coalitions, promote regional stability, support the development of indigenous counterdrug law enforcement capabilities, and serve as role models for militaries in emerging democracies. With countries that are neither staunch friends nor known foes, military cooperation can serve as a positive means of building bridges between the military leaderships of different nations. These links enhance security relationships between the nations today and will contribute to improved relations tomorrow. At the same time, we also remain firmly committed to human rights and we will ensure our military forces do not knowingly train or assist units that have committed a gross violation of human rights.

Maintaining our overseas presence enhances our understanding of the military developments within various regions of the world. Relevant observations add to our larger geo-political understanding of potential areas for instability or threats to our national interests and help select our optimal avenue of response; diplomatic, economic, or military. It reassures our allies and promotes regional stability. It gives substance to our security commitments, helps prevent the development of power vacuums and instability, and contributes to deterrence by demonstrating our determination to defend U.S., allied, and friendly interests in critical regions. Having credible combat forces forward deployed in peacetime also better positions the United States to respond rapidly to crises, permitting them to be first on the scene. Equally essential is effective global power projection, which is key to the flexibility demanded of our forces and provides options for responding to potential crises and conflicts even when we have no permanent presence or a limited infrastructure in a region.

Just as U.S. engagement overall must be selective -- focusing on the threats and opportunities most relevant to our interests and applying our resources where we can make the greatest difference -- so too must our use of the Armed Forces for engagement be equally discerning. Engagement activities must be carefully managed to prevent erosion of our military's current and long-term readiness for larger-scale contingencies. The Defense Department's theater engagement planning process, which was approved by the President in 1997, helps ensure that military engagement activities are prioritized within theaters, and balanced against available resources. In short, we must prioritize military engagement activities to ensure the readiness of our Armed Forces to carry out crisis response and warfighting missions, as well as to ensure that we can sustain an appropriate level of engagement activities over the long term.

Our ability to deter potential adversaries in peacetime rests on several factors, particularly on our demonstrated will and ability to uphold our security commitments when they are challenged. We have earned this reputation through both our declaratory policy, which clearly communicates costs to potential adversaries, and our credible warfighting capability across the full spectrum of conflict. This capability is embodied in four ways; ready forces and equipment strategically stationed or deployed forward, forces in the United States at the appropriate level of readiness to deploy when needed, our ability to maintain access to critical regions and infrastructure overseas, and our demonstrated ability to form and lead effective military coalitions.

We must continue to improve our program to combat terrorism in the areas of antiterrorism, counterterrorism, consequence management, and intelligence support to deter terrorism. We will deter terrorism through the increased antiterrorism readiness of our installations and forward forces, enhanced training and awareness of military personnel, and the development of comprehensive theater engagement plans. In counterterrorism, because terrorist organizations may not be deterred by traditional means, we must ensure a robust capability to accurately attribute the source of attacks against the United States or its citizens, and to respond effectively and decisively to protect our national interests. U.S. armed forces possess a tailored range of options to respond to terrorism directed at U.S. citizens, interests, and property. In the event of a terrorist incident, our consequence management ability to significantly mitigate injury and damage may likely deter future attacks. Finally, we will continue to improve the timeliness and accuracy of intelligence support to commanders, which will also enhance our ability to deter terrorism.

Our nuclear deterrent posture is one example of how U.S. military capabilities are used effectively to deter aggression and coercion against U.S. interests. Nuclear weapons serve as a guarantor of our security commitments to allies and a disincentive to those who would contemplate developing or otherwise acquiring their own WMD capability. Those who threaten the United States or its allies with WMD should have no doubt that any such attack would meet an overwhelming and devastating response. Our military planning for the possible employment of U.S. strategic nuclear weapons is focused on deterring a nuclear war and it emphasizes the survivability of our nuclear systems, infrastructure, and command, control, and communications systems necessary to endure a preemptive attack yet still deliver an overwhelming response. Another key element of the U.S. nuclear deterrent strategy is ensuring the National Command Authorities have a survivable and endurable command, control, and communications capability through which to execute the mission and direct nuclear forces during all phases of a nuclear war. The United States will continue to maintain a robust triad of strategic nuclear forces sufficient to deter any potential adversaries who may have or seek access to nuclear forces -- to convince them that seeking a nuclear advantage or resorting to nuclear weapons would be futile. In addition, some U.S. non-strategic nuclear forces are forward deployed in NATO to demonstrate the political commitment of the United States to the long-term viability of NATO and European security. We must also ensure the continued viability of the infrastructure that supports U.S. nuclear forces and weapons. The Stockpile Stewardship Program will provide high confidence in the safety and reliability of our nuclear weapons under the Comprehensive Nuclear Test Ban Treaty.

The Department of Defense's Counterproliferation Initiative provides another example of how U.S. military capabilities are used effectively to deter aggression and coercion against U.S. interests. Under this initiative, we are preparing our own forces and working with allies to ensure that we can prevail on the battlefield despite the threatened or actual use of NBC weapons by adversaries.

The United States is committed to preserving internationally recognized freedom of navigation on -- and overflight of -- the world's oceans, which are critical to the future strength of our nation and the maintenance of global stability. Freedom of navigation and overflight are essential to our economic security and for the worldwide movement and sustainment of U.S. military forces. These freedoms are codified in the United Nations Convention on the Law of the Sea, which the President submitted to the Senate in 1994 for advice and consent to ratification. In addition to lending the certainty of the rule of law to an area critical to our national security, the Convention preserves our leadership in global ocean policy. Thus, the Law of the Sea Convention buttresses the strategic advantages that the United States gains from being a global power, and ratification of the Convention remains a high priority.

Quality people -- civilian and military -- are our most critical asset in implementing our defense activities. The quality of our men and women in uniform will be the deciding factor in future military operations where the operation and maintenance of information systems and advanced technology become ever more important. We must ensure that we remain the most fully prepared and best trained military force in the world. Accordingly, we will continue to place the highest priority and bear the costs associated with programs that support recruiting, retention, quality of life, training, equipping and educating our personnel.

International Law Enforcement Cooperation

Certain criminal threats to our national security are international in nature. Transnational threats include terrorism, drug and migrant smuggling, and other international crime. The rise in the frequency and intensity of these threats makes it incumbent upon U.S. and foreign law enforcement and judicial authorities to cooperate in an innovative manner. The President's International Crime Control Strategy prescribes the role of overseas law enforcement presence in establishing and sustaining working relationships with foreign law enforcement agencies; keeping crime away from our shores; enabling extradition; and solving serious U.S. crimes.

The Department of State and U.S. federal law enforcement agencies continue to assist law enforcement agencies in Central and Eastern Europe and East Asia through cooperative centers established in Hungary and Thailand known as the International Law Enforcement Academies (ILEAs). The ILEA initiative is a multinational effort organized by the United States, the host nations, and other international training partners to provide mutual assistance and law enforcement training.

Environmental and Health Initiatives

The President has said, "Our natural security must be seen as part of our national security." Decisions today regarding the environment and natural resources can affect our security for generations. Environmental threats do not heed national borders; environmental perils overseas and environmental crime pose long-term dangers to U.S. security and well being. Natural resource scarcities can trigger and exacerbate conflict, and phenomena such as climate change, toxic pollution, ocean dumping, and ozone depletion directly threaten the health and well-being of Americans and all other individuals on Earth.

Responding firmly to environmental threats remains a part of mainstream American foreign policy. America's leadership was essential for agreement on the Kyoto Protocol -- the first binding agreement among the world's industrialized nations to reduce greenhouse gas emissions. America also brokered key international agreements on toxic chemicals -- such as persistent organic pollutants, environmental aspects of biotechnology, the ozone layer, and endangered marine life. America's insistence on high environmental standards in its own trade agreements, in international financial institutions, and in bilateral export credit and development assistance programs similarly demonstrates to the rest of the international community that growing economies and clean environments do go hand-in-hand. America also provided leadership in the Global Environment Facility and in bilateral programs for clean energy development, as well as conservation of biological diversity and endangered ecosystems such as tropical forests.

With globalization, the free flow of people and goods across national borders continues to increase rapidly with each passing year. This interdependence has caused diseases and health risks around the world to become matters of both U.S. national and international security. The United States promotes international cooperation on health issues because it reduces the threat of diseases to Americans, and because global international economic development, democratization, and political stability are predicated in part on the health of populations worldwide.

Beyond these general concerns, a number of specific international health issues are critical for our national security. Because a growing proportion of our national food supply is coming from international sources, assuring the safety of the food we consume must be a priority. The Administration has announced new and stronger programs to ensure the safety of imported as well as domestic foods, to be overseen by the President's Council on Food Safety. New and emerging infections such as drug-resistant tuberculosis and the Ebola virus can move with the speed of jet travel. We are actively engaged with the international health community as well as the World Health Organization to stop the spread of these dangerous diseases.

Combating the global epidemic of HIV/AIDS has been a top international health priority in recent years. AIDS is now the number one cause of death on the continent of Africa. The United States led the United Nations Security Council in holding its first-ever session on AIDS in Africa and has committed to efforts to accelerate the development and delivery of vaccines for AIDS and other diseases that disproportionately affect the developing world. We also have promoted efforts by African national governments to provide AIDS awareness education to their military members who travel widely around the continent; and led the G-8's decision to link debt relief to HIV/AIDS prevention and other such programs.

Population issues have also been a health priority garnering renewed focus internationally. The Administration has re-established U.S. leadership on international population issues by expanding quality reproductive health care. This includes voluntary family planning services for women and men around the world; improving the political, economic, and social status of women; and enhancing educational opportunities for women and girls.

Responding to Threats and Crises

Because our efforts to shape the international environment alone cannot guarantee the security we seek, the United States must be able to respond at home and abroad to the full spectrum of threats and crises that may arise. Since our resources are finite, we must be selective in our responses, focusing on challenges that most directly affect our interests and engaging when and where we can have the greatest positive impact. We must use the most appropriate tool or combination of tools -- diplomacy, public diplomacy, economic measures, law enforcement, intelligence, military operations, and others. We act in alliance or partnership when others share our interests, but will act unilaterally when compelling national interests so demand.

Efforts to deter an adversary -- be it an aggressor nation, terrorist group or criminal organization -- can become the leading edge of crisis response. In this sense, deterrence straddles the line between shaping the international environment and responding to crises. Deterrence in crisis generally involves demonstrating the United States' commitment to a particular country or interest by enhancing our warfighting capability in the theater. Our forward and rotationally deployed forces are the embodiment of our continuous commitment to our overseas partners and act as the first line of deterrence, providing the necessary inroads to access and influence to help defuse crisis situations.

Our ability to respond to the full spectrum of threats requires that we have the best-trained, best-equipped, most effective armed forces in the world. Our strategy requires that we have highly capable ground, air, naval, special operations, and space forces supported by a range of enabling capabilities including strategic mobility and Command, Control, Communications, Computers, Intelligence, Surveillance, and Reconnaissance (C41SR). Maintaining our superior forces requires developing superior technology, and exploiting it to the fullest extent.

Strategic mobility is critical to our ability to augment forces already present in the region with the projection of additional forces for both domestic and international crisis response. This agility in response is key to successful American leadership and engagement. Access to sufficient fleets of aircraft, ships, vehicles, and trains, as well as bases, ports, pre-positioned equipment, and other infrastructure will of course be an imperative if we are to deploy and sustain U.S. and multinational forces in regions of interest to us.

We are committed to maintaining U.S. preeminence in space. Unimpeded access to and use of space is a vital national interest -- essential for protecting U.S. national security, promoting our prosperity, and ensuring our well-being. Consistent with our international obligations, we will deter threats to our interests in space, counter hostile efforts against U.S. access to and use of space, and maintain the ability to counter space systems and services that could be used for hostile purposes against our military forces, command and control systems, or other critical capabilities. We will maintain our technological superiority in space systems, and sustain a robust U.S. space industry and a strong, forward-looking research base. We also will continue efforts to prevent the spread of weapons of mass destruction to space, and will continue to pursue global partnerships addressing space-related scientific, economic, environmental, and security issues.

We also are committed to maintaining information superiority -- the capability to collect, process, and disseminate an uninterrupted flow of information while exploiting and/or denying an adversary's ability to do the same. Operational readiness, as well as the command and control of forces, relies increasingly on information systems and technology. We must keep pace with rapidly evolving information technology so that we can cultivate and harvest the promise of the knowledge that comes from this information superiority, sharing that knowledge among U.S. forces and coalition partners while exploiting the shortfalls in our adversaries' information capabilities.

Protecting the Homeland

Emerging threats to our homeland by both state and non-state actors may be more likely in the future as our potential adversaries strike against vulnerable civilian targets in the United States to avoid direct confrontation with our military forces. Such acts represent a new dimension of asymmetric threats to our national security. Easier access to the critical technical expertise and technologies enables both state and non-state actors to harness increasingly destructive power with greater ease. In response to such threats, the United States has embarked on a comprehensive strategy to prevent, deter, disrupt, and when necessary, effectively respond to the myriad of threats to our homeland that we will face.

National Missile Defense

The Clinton Administration is committed to the development of a limited National Missile Defense (NMD) system designed to counter the emerging ballistic missile threat from states that threaten international peace and security. On September 1, 2000, the President announced that while the technology for NMD was promising, the system as a whole is not yet proven, and thus he was not prepared to proceed with the deployment of a limited NMD system. The President has instead asked the Secretary of Defense to continue a robust program of development and testing. The Administration recognizes the relationship among the ABM Treaty, strategic stability, and the START process, and is committed to working with Russia on any modifications to the ABM Treaty required to deploy a limited NMD. An NMD system, if deployed, would be part of a larger strategy to preserve and enhance peace and security.

In making this decision, the President considered the threat, cost, technical feasibility and impact overall on our national security of proceeding with NMD, including the impact on arms control and relations with Russia, China, and our allies. He considered a thorough technical review by the Department of Defense as well as the advice of his top national security advisors.

The Pentagon has made progress on developing a system that can address the emerging missile threat. But, at this time, we do not have sufficient information to conclude that it can work reliably under realistic conditions. Critical elements of the program, such as the booster rocket for the missile interceptor, have not been tested; and there are also questions to be resolved about the ability of the system to deal with countermeasures. The President made clear that we should not move forward until we have further confidence that the system will work and until we have made every reasonable diplomatic effort to minimize the international consequences. In the interim, the Pentagon will continue the development and testing of the NMD system. That effort is still at an early stage: three of the nineteen, planned intercept tests have been held so far. Additional ground tests and simulations will also take place.

The development of our NMD is part of the Administration's comprehensive national security strategy to prevent potential adversaries from acquiring and/or threatening the United States with such weapons. Arms control agreements with Russia are an important part of this strategy because they ensure stability and predictability between the United States and Russia, promote the dismantling of nuclear weapons, and help complete the transition from confrontation to cooperation with Russia. The 1972 Anti-Ballistic Missile (ABM) Treaty limits anti-missile defenses according to the following principle: neither side should deploy defenses that would undermine the other's nuclear deterrent, and thus tempt the other to strike first in a crisis or take countermeasures that would make both our countries less secure. The President's decision not to deploy a limited NMD system will provide additional time to pursue with Russia the goal of adapting the ABM Treaty to permit the deployment of a limited NMD that would not undermine strategic stability. The United States will also continue to consult with allies and hold dialogues with other states.

In August 1999, President Clinton decided that the initial NMD architecture would include: 100 ground-based interceptors deployed in Alaska, one ABM radar in Alaska, and five upgraded early warning radar. This approach is the fastest, most affordable, and most technologically mature approach to fielding an NMD system capable of protecting all 50 states against projected emerging threats.

On July 23, 1999, President Clinton signed H.R. 4, the "National Missile Defense Act of 1999," stating that it is the policy of the United States to deploy an effective NMD system as soon as technologically possible. The legislation includes two amendments supported by the Administration. The first makes clear that any NMD deployment must be subject to the authorization and appropriations process, and thus that no decision on deployment has been made. The second amendment states that it is the policy of the United States to seek continued negotiated reductions in Russian nuclear forces, putting Congress on record as continuing to support negotiated reductions in strategic nuclear arms, reaffirming the Administration's position that missile defense policy must take into account important arms control and nuclear nonproliferation objectives.

Countering Foreign Intelligence Collection

The United States is a primary target of foreign intelligence services due to our military, scientific, technological and economic preeminence. Foreign intelligence services aggressively seek information about U.S. political and military intentions and capabilities. As the rapidity of global technological change accelerates and the gap with some nations has widened, these countries' foreign intelligence agencies are stepping up their efforts to collect classified or sensitive information on U.S. weapons systems, U.S. intelligence collection methods, emerging technologies with military applications, and related technical methods. Such information enables potential adversaries to counter U.S. political and military objectives, develop sophisticated weapons more quickly and efficiently, and develop countermeasures against U.S. weapons and related technical methods. Intelligence collection against U.S. economic, commercial, and proprietary information enables foreign states and corporations to obtain shortcuts to industrial development and improve their competitiveness against U.S. corporations in global markets. Although difficult to quantify, economic and industrial espionage results in the loss of millions of dollars and thousands of jobs annually.

To protect sensitive national security information, it is critical for us to effectively counter the collection efforts of foreign intelligence services and non-state actors through vigorous counterintelligence efforts and security programs. Over the last six years, we have created new counterintelligence mechanisms to address economic and industrial espionage and have implemented procedures to improve coordination among intelligence, counterintelligence and law enforcement agencies. These measures have considerably strengthened our ability to counter the foreign intelligence collection threat. We will continue to refine and enhance our counterintelligence capabilities as we enter the 21st century.

Dramatic geopolitical changes that continue into the first decade of the 21 s' century increase rather than lessen the need to protect sensitive national security information. Some of this information is classified while some is unclassified but sensitive due to its relationship to, or impact upon, our critical infrastructure. Increased threats to our cyber security and the inadvertent or deliberate disclosure of sensitive information underscore the necessity for the National Security Community to have reliable, timely, and trusted information available to those who both need it and are authorized to have it. During the last five years we have established a set of security countermeasures policies, practices, procedures, and programs for a rational, fair, forward looking, and cost-effective security system. More needs to be done, however, and efforts will continue in providing a better synchronized, integrated and interoperable programs for personnel security, physical security, technical security, operational security, education and awareness, information assurance, classification management, industrial security, and counterintelligence.

Combating Terrorism

The United States has mounted an aggressive response to terrorism. Our strategy pressures terrorists, deters attacks, and responds forcefully to terrorist acts. It combines enhanced law enforcement and intelligence efforts; vigorous diplomacy and economic sanctions; and, when necessary, military force. Domestically, we seek to stop terrorists before they act, and eliminate their support networks and financing. Overseas, we seek to eliminate terrorist sanctuaries; counter state and non-governmental support for terrorism; help other governments improve their physical and political counterterrorism, antiterrorism, and consequence management efforts; tighten embassy and military facility security; and protect U.S. citizens living and traveling abroad. Whether at home or abroad, we will respond to terrorism through defensive readiness of our facilities and personnel, and the ability of our terrorism consequence management efforts to mitigate injury and damage.

Our strategy requires us to both prevent and, if necessary, respond to terrorism. Prevention -- which includes intelligence collection, breaking up cells, and limiting the movement, planning, and organization of terrorists -- entails more unknowns and its effectiveness will never be fully proven or appreciated, but it is certainly the preferable path. For example, as a result of the quiet cooperation with some of our allies and among federal authorities, agencies, and local law enforcement, planned terrorist attacks within the United States and against U.S. interests abroad during the millennium celebration were thwarted. A major aspect of our prevention efforts is bolstering the political will and security capabilities of those states that are on the front lines to terrorist threats and that are disproportionately impacted by the expanding threat. This coalition of nations is imperative to the international effort to contain and fight the terrorism that threatens American interests.

Avenues of international trade provide a highway for the tools and weapons of international terrorists. The same sophisticated transportation network that can efficiently, safely, and reliably move people and goods is also equally attractive to those whose motives may be hostile, dangerous, or criminal. Systems that promote efficiency, volume and speed, fueling economic prosperity, create new challenges in the balance between policing and facilitating the transnational movements of people and goods. Globalization and electronic commerce transcend conventional borders, fast rendering traditional border security measures at air, land, and sea ports of entry ineffective or obsolete. Despite the challenges, we are developing tools to close off this avenue for terrorists. In this new environment, prudent, reasonable, and affordable security measures will require an approach transcending any particular transportation node or sector. The International Trade Data System (ITDS), already in initial implementation pilot testing, was created to foster an integrated system to electronically collect, use, and disseminate international trade and transportation data. By transcending transportation nodes and sectors, efforts like the ITDS project will foreclose opportunities terrorists may believe are emerging with globalization.

When terrorism occurs, despite our best efforts, we can neither forget the crime nor ever give up on bringing its perpetrators to justice. We make no concessions to terrorists. Since 1993, a dozen terrorist fugitives have been apprehended overseas and rendered, formally or informally, to the United States to answer for their crimes. These include the perpetrators of the World Trade Center bombing, the attack outside CIA headquarters, and an attack on a Pan Am flight more than 18 years ago. In 1998, the U.S. Armed Forces carried out strikes against a chemical weapons target and an active terrorist base operated by Usama bin Ladin, whose terror network had carried out bombings of American embassies in Nairobi and Dar es Salaam and planned still other attacks against Americans. We will likewise pursue the criminals responsible for the attack on the USS Cole in Yemen.

Whenever possible, we use law enforcement, diplomatic, and economic tools to wage the fight against terrorism. But there have been, and will be, times when those tools are not enough. As long as terrorists continue to target American citizens, we reserve the right to act in self-defense by striking at their bases and those who sponsor, assist, or actively support them, as we have done over the years in different countries.

Fighting terrorism requires a substantial commitment of financial, human, and political resources. Since 1993, both the FBI's counterterrorism budget and the number of FBI agents assigned to counterterrorism have more than doubled. The President has also created and filled the post of National Coordinator for Security, Infrastructure Protection, and Counterterrorism. Three presidential directives now coordinate the efforts of senior counterterrorism personnel from various government agencies in dealing with WMD and other threats at home. The FBI and the State Department, respectively, operate Rapid Deployment Teams and interagency Foreign Emergency Support Teams to deploy quickly to scenes of terrorist incidents worldwide.

However, it is not only the response capabilities that need significant resources. It is our preventive efforts, such as active diplomatic and military engagement, political pressure, economic sanctions, and bolstering allies' political and security capabilities, that also require strong financial support in order to squeeze terrorists before they act. Providing political support and economic assistance to front line states and other allies impacted by this threat expands the circle of nations fighting against threats to the United States. These preventive measures are an important partner to our counterterrorism response efforts.

We must continue to devote the necessary resources for America's strategy to combat terrorism, which integrates preventive and responsive measures and encompasses a graduated scale of enhanced law enforcement and intelligence gathering, vigorous diplomacy, and, where needed, military action.

Domestic Preparedness Against Weapons of Mass Destruction

Defending the United States against weapons of mass destruction is a top national security priority. In October 1998, the President signed into law legislation criminalizing the unjustified accumulation of dangerous chemicals, thereby enhancing the ability of law enforcement to prevent potentially catastrophic terrorist acts by allowing enforcement action before the chemicals are weaponized. Additionally, concerted efforts have been undertaken to mitigate the consequences of a WMD attack.

The Federal Government, in coordination with state and local authorities, will respond rapidly and decisively to any terrorist incident in the United States involving WMD. Increased preparedness at home is critical to defending against, and responding to, such unconventional threats. The Administration developed a Five-Year Interagency Counterterrorism and Technology Crime Plan to address these issues.

Established in 1998, a standing Weapons of Mass Destruction Preparedness Interagency Working Group, chaired by the National Coordinator, addresses current and future requirements of local, state, and federal authorities that are directly responsible for the WMD crisis and consequence management efforts. In coordinating the interagency process and cooperation between these three levels of government, several initiatives are now in place to better prepare the United States against a WMD incident. These initiatives include equipping and training first responders in the 157 largest metropolitan areas across the nation to prepare for, and defend against, chemical, biological, or nuclear weapons of mass destruction attacks; renovating the public health surveillance system; and establishing civilian medical stockpiles of vaccines and antibiotics.

Critical Infrastructure Protection

An extraordinarily sophisticated information technology (IT) infrastructure fuels America's economy and national security. Critical infrastructures, including telecommunications, energy, finance, transportation, water, and emergency services, form a bedrock upon which the success of all our endeavors -- economic, social, and military -- depend. These infrastructures are highly interconnected, both physically and by the manner in which they rely upon information technology and the national information infrastructure. This trend toward increasing interdependence has accelerated in recent years with the advent of the Information Age.

At the same time that the IT revolution has led to substantially more interconnected infrastructures with generally greater centralized control, the advent of "just in time" business practices has reduced margins for error for infrastructure owners and operators. In addition, the trend toward deregulation and growth of competition in key infrastructures has understandably eroded the willingness of owners and operators to pay for spare capacity that traditionally served a useful "shock absorber' role in cushioning key infrastructures from failures. Finally, the increase in the number of mergers among infrastructure providers has increased the pressure for further reductions in spare capacity as managers seek to reduce overhead and wring "excess" costs out of merged companies.

As with the 1993 World Trade Center bombing, ongoing hostile hacker attacks, and cyber conflicts between China and Taiwan have shown, asymmetric warfare against the United States will likely grow. We must understand the vulnerabilities and interdependencies of our infrastructures, accept that such attacks know no international boundaries, and work to mitigate potential problems.

In January 2000, the President launched the National Plan for Information Systems Protection and announced new budget proposals for critical infrastructure protection. Specific new proposals included the Federal Cyber Systems Training and Education program to offer IT education in exchange for federal service; an intrusion detection network for the Department of Defense and for federal civilian agencies; and the Institute for Information Infrastructure Protection, an innovative public/private partnership to fill key gaps in critical infrastructure protection R&D. The Institute represented part of a 32% increase that were proposed for computer security research and development efforts for the FY 2001 budget.

Implementing the proposals of the National Plan, as well as other future projects, will contribute to our economic competitiveness, military strength, and general public health and safety. These proposals will also protect the ability of state and local governments to maintain order and deliver minimum essential public services while also working with the private sector to ensure the orderly functioning of the economy and the delivery of vital services.

The National Infrastructure Protection Center (NIPC), founded in 1998 under Presidential Decision Directive 63, is the national focal point for warning, analysis, and response regarding threats to the infrastructures. Over the past two years it has provided warnings to the private sector, federal, state, and local governments regarding infrastructure threats. It has also coordinated numerous investigations of destructive computer viruses, computer intrusions against United States Government and private IT systems, and denial of service attacks both in the United States and overseas.

Some aspects of our critical infrastructure, such as the various transportation systems, are not commonly associated with the trends of globalization and technological change, but nonetheless are being dramatically affected by them. For example, the Marine Transportation System, which consists of waterways, ports, and their intermodal connections, vessels, vehicles and system users, provides American businesses with critical competitive access to suppliers and markets that will be key to maintaining our nation's role as a global power. Threats to this and other transportation systems will drive new security imperatives that we must continue to balance with the need for speed and efficiency. In any case, ensuring the long-term health of these traditional aspects of our critical infrastructure must remain a priority even as we look to new technologies to improve other aspects of our infrastructures and provide other competitive advantages.

Most importantly, the Federal Government cannot protect critical infrastructures alone. The private sector owns and operates the vast majority of these infrastructures. Protecting critical infrastructure, therefore, requires the Federal Government to build partnerships with the private sector in all areas -- from business and higher education, to law enforcement, to R&D. The Secretary of Commerce and industry leaders -- mostly from Fortune 500 companies -- are leading the Partnership for Critical Infrastructure Security. The Attorney General has teamed up with the Information Technology Association of America to promote industry-government cooperation against cyber crime through the Cyber Citizen project. The NIPC, meanwhile, is establishing cooperative relationships between industry and law enforcement through its InfraGard initiative.

Some segments of our critical infrastructures have not historically devoted significant resources to protection from threats other than those caused by natural means. As a result, we are building a strong foundation for continued protection of our critical infrastructures. The public and private sectors must work together to conduct R&D in infrastructure protection and interdependencies, increase investment in training and educating cyber-security practitioners (to include building an adequate base of researchers in this new discipline), and find innovative technical, policy, and legal solutions that protect our infrastructures and preserve our civil rights.

National Security Emergency Preparedness

U.S. Continuity of Government and Continuity of Operations programs remain a top national security priority into the 21st century. They preserve the capability to govern, lead, and perform essential functions and services to meet essential defense and civilian needs. Together with other security, critical infrastructure protection, and counterterrorism programs, Continuity of Government and Continuity of Operations programs remain an important hedge against current and emerging threats, and future uncertainties.

We will do all we can to deter and prevent destructive and threatening forces such as terrorism, NBC weapons use, disruption of our critical infrastructures, and regional or state-centered threats from endangering our citizens. But if an emergency occurs, we must be prepared to respond effectively at home and abroad to protect lives and property, mobilize the personnel, resources, and capabilities necessary to effectively handle the emergency, and ensure the survival of our institutions and infrastructures. To this end, comprehensive, all-hazard emergency planning by Federal departments, agencies and the military, as well as a strong and responsive industrial and technology base, will be maintained as crucial national security emergency preparedness requirements.

Fighting Drug Trafficking and Other International Crime

Broad ranges of criminal activities that originate overseas threaten the safety and well being of the American people.

Drug Trafficking. Drug use and its damaging consequences cost our society over $110 billion per year and poison the schools and neighborhoods where our youth learn and play. Aggressive law enforcement is dramatically weakening the domestic perpetrators of organized crime who have controlled America's drug trade for much of the past century. Today, international drug syndicates based abroad challenge us. The criminals who run the international drug trade continue to diversify and seek new markets in the United

States -- moving beyond large cities into smaller communities and even rural towns. All Americans, regardless of economic, geographic, or other position in society, feel the effects of drug use.

The National Drug Control Strategy, both at home and abroad, integrates prevention and treatment with law enforcement and interdiction efforts. We aim to cut illegal drug use and availability in the United States by 50% by 2007, and reduce the health and social consequences of drug use and trafficking by 25% over the same period.

Domestically, we have engaged in a wide range of treatment and prevention efforts. We seek to educate and enable our youth to reject illegal drugs, increase the safety of U.S. citizens by substantially reducing drug-related crime and violence; reduce health and social costs to the public of illegal drug use; reduce domestic cultivation of cannabis and production of methamphetamines and other synthetic drugs; and shield America's air, land, and sea frontiers from the drug threat.

The Drug-Free Community Support program and the Drug-Free Schools and Communities program promote citizen participation in anti-drug efforts and help to provide drug-free learning environments for our children. The Office of National Drug Control Policy is leading the implementation of a $2 billion, multi-year, science-based, national media campaign on the consequences of youth drug use. In the law enforcement arena, we have assisted communities in their law enforcement efforts; are committed to stemming the flow of drugs into our country; and have enhanced coordination among Federal, state, and local law enforcement agencies to arrest and prosecute drug traffickers and abusers. Concerted efforts by the public, all levels of government, and the private sector, together with other governments, private groups, and international organizations will be required for our strategy to succeed.

Internationally, our strategy recognizes that the most effective counterdrug operations are mounted at the source where illegal drugs are grown and produced. Our efforts therefore center on supply reduction in major drug exporting countries. In these "source nations," we act to bolster the capabilities of governments to help them reduce cultivation by eradicating drug crops, develop alternative crops, destroy drug labs, and control chemicals used in illegal drug production. As a second line of defense, in the transit zone between source regions and the U.S. border, we detect, monitor, and communicate with partner nations on the movement of suspicious surface, sea, and air traffic outside the United States. We support interdiction programs to halt the shipment of illicit drugs. In concert with allies abroad, we pursue prosecution of major drug traffickers, dismantling drug trafficking organizations, prevention of money laundering, and elimination of criminal financial support networks.

In an example of such cooperative effort, the United States is providing $1.3 billion in support for Plan Colombia, President Andres Pastrana's effort to fight Colombian drug trafficking and strengthen democracy, as well as promote legitimate economic endeavors in Colombia. Since Colombian drug traffickers supply approximately 90% of the cocaine used in the United States, U.S. assistance to Plan Colombia's interdiction, eradication, and alternative crop development efforts will be necessary if we are to stem this deadly drug's flow into the United States. As an additional measure, we continue to strongly support interdiction programs to halt the flow of drugs across the U.S. border either by independent means or exploiting the U.S. transportation system.

Other International Crime. Economic globalization increasingly makes all nations and peoples vulnerable to various unlawful activities that impede rational business decisions and fair competition in a market economy. Such activities include, but are not limited to, extortion, corruption, migrant smuggling, trafficking in persons, money laundering, counterfeiting, credit card and other financial fraud, and intellectual property theft. Many of these activities tend to impede or disrupt the safe and secure international movement of passengers and goods across international lines. They also attack the integrity and reliability of international financial systems. Corruption and extortion activities by organized crime groups can even undermine the integrity of government and imperil fragile democracies. And, the failure of governments to effectively control international crime rings within their borders or their willingness to harbor international criminals endangers global stability. There must be no safe haven where criminals can roam free, beyond the reach of our extradition and legal assistance treaties.

Open markets must be preserved, laws and regulations governing financial institutions must be standardized, and international law enforcement cooperation in the financial sector must be improved for the benefits of economic globalization to be preserved.

The United States is implementing a number of initiatives and strategies tailored to combat various forms of international crime. For example, we launched the National Money Laundering Strategy, under which the Departments of Treasury and Justice work to disrupt illegal profit flows to organized crime groups. The Presidential Decision Directive on International Organized Crime directs close coordination among Federal agencies to identify, target, and disrupt the activities of criminal groups, and the President's International Crime Control Strategy establishes the broad goals and implementing objectives for this effort. Finally, in December 2000, the United States published its first-ever comprehensive International Crime Threat Assessment detailing criminal activities around the globe that impact our national security.

The United States is pursuing efforts to combat international crimes that are economic in origin, but the effects of which transcend economics. They include crimes that result in the contamination of the environment, such as the illegal international movement of chloro-fluorocarbons (CFCs) that attack the ozone layer, thereby endangering all life on earth. They also include crimes that threaten the world's diversity through illegal trafficking in endangered and threatened species of flora and fauna. The United States continues to work with nations around the world to counter these crimes.

Smaller-Scale Contingencies

Smaller-scale contingency (SSC) operations encompass the full range of military operations short of major theater warfare, including peacekeeping operations, enforcing embargoes and no-fly zones, evacuating U.S. citizens, reinforcing key allies, neutralizing NBC weapons facilities, supporting counterdrug operations, protecting freedom of navigation in international waters, providing disaster relief and humanitarian assistance, coping with mass migration, and engaging in information operations. These challenging operations are likely to arise frequently and require significant commitments of human and fiscal resources over time. These operations also put a premium on the ability of the U.S. military to work closely and effectively with other United States Government agencies, non-governmental organizations, regional and international security organizations and coalition partners.

In general, SSC operations are aimed at checking aggression and addressing local and regional crises before they escalate or spread. Thus, while SSCs may involve other than "vital" national security interests, resolving SSCs gives us the chance to prevent greater and costlier conflicts that might well threaten U.S. vital interests.

The United States need not take on sole responsibility for operations and expenditures in SSCs. In fact, we have encouraged and supported friends and allies' assumption of both participatory and leadership roles in regional conflicts. Such encouragement, in theory, constitutes a fruitful middle ground between inaction and conflict. In practice, the United States has recently played a role in a number of successful coalition operations. These include participating in NATO-led Bosnia and Kosovo operations with predominantly European troop participation; providing logistical, intelligence, and other support to operations in East Timor; and supporting the United Nations' and Economic Community of West African States' leadership roles in seeking peace for Sierra Leone.

Coalition efforts in SSCs raise the critical question of command and control. Under no circumstances will the President ever relinquish his constitutional command authority over U.S. forces. However, there may be times in the future, just as in the past, when it is in our interest to place U.S. forces under the temporary operational control of a competent allied or United Nations commander.

There is an important role for the United Nations as a tool in managing conflict. UN peacekeeping operations can be a very effective alternative to direct intervention by the United States. The Brahimi report on peacekeeping reform offers many good recommendations that, if implemented, can make this tool even more effective as an instrument of policy.

As in regional conflict, conducting smaller-scale contingencies means confronting new threats such as terrorism, information attack, computer network operations, and the use or threat of use of weapons of mass destruction. United States forces must also remain prepared to withdraw from contingency operations if they are needed in the event of a major theater war. Accordingly, we must continue to train, equip, and organize U.S. forces to be capable of performing multiple missions at any given time.

Major Theater Warfare

Fighting and winning major theater wars is the ultimate test of our Armed Forces -- a test at which they must always succeed. For the foreseeable future, the United States, preferably in concert with allies, must have the capability to deter and, if deterrence fails, defeat large-scale, cross-border aggression in two distant theaters in overlapping time frames. Maintaining a two major theater war capability reassures our friends and allies and makes coalition relationships with the United States more attractive. It deters opportunism elsewhere when we are heavily involved in deterring or defeating aggression in one theater, or while conducting multiple smaller-scale contingencies and engagement activities in other theaters. It also provides a hedge against the possibility that we might encounter threats larger or more difficult than expected. A strategy for deterring and defeating aggression in two theaters ensures that we maintain the capability and flexibility to meet unknown future threats, while continued global engagement helps preclude such threats from developing.

Fighting and winning major theater wars entails three challenging requirements. First, we must maintain the ability to rapidly defeat initial enemy advances short of the enemy's objectives in two theaters, in close succession. We must maintain this ability to ensure that we can seize the initiative, minimize territory lost before an invasion is halted, and ensure the integrity of our warfighting coalitions. Failure to defeat initial enemy advances rapidly would make the subsequent campaign to evict enemy forces from captured territory more difficult, lengthy and costly, and could undermine U.S. credibility and increase the risk of conflict elsewhere.

Second, the United States must be prepared to fight and win under conditions where an adversary may use asymmetric means against us -- unconventional approaches that avoid or undermine our strengths while exploiting our vulnerabilities. Because of our conventional military dominance, adversaries are likely to use asymmetric means, such as NBC weapons, information operations, attacks on our critical infrastructure, or terrorism. Such asymmetric attacks could be used to disrupt the critical logistics pipeline -- from its origins in the United States, along sea and air routes, at in-transit refueling and staging bases, to its termination at airfields, seaports, and supply depots in theater -- as well as our forces deployed in the field. The threat of NBC attacks against U.S. forces in theater or U.S. territory could be used in an attempt to deter U.S. military action in defense of its allies and other security interests.

We are enhancing the preparedness of our Armed Forces to effectively conduct sustained operations despite the presence, threat, or use of NBC weapons. These efforts include development, procurement, and deployment of theater missile defense systems to protect forward-deployed military personnel, as well as enhanced passive defenses against chemical and biological weapons, improved intelligence collection and counterforce capabilities, heightened security awareness and force protection measures worldwide. We are also enhancing our ability to defend against hostile information operations, which could, in the future, take the form of a full-scale, strategic information attack against our critical national infrastructures, government, and economy -- as well as attacks directed against our military forces.

Third, our military must also be able to transition to fighting major theater wars from a posture of global engagement -- from substantial levels of peacetime engagement overseas as well as multiple concurrent smaller-scale contingency operations. Withdrawing from such operations would pose significant political and operational challenges. Options available to the National Command Authorities (NCA) may include backfilling those forces withdrawn from contingency operations or substituting for forces committed to such operations. Ultimately, however, the United States must accept a degree of risk associated with withdrawing from contingency operations and engagement activities in order to reduce the greater risk incurred if we failed to respond adequately to major theater wars.

The Decision to Employ Military Forces

The decision whether to use force is dictated first and foremost by our national interests. In those specific areas where our **vital interests** are at stake, our use of force will be decisive and, if necessary, unilateral.

In situations posing a threat to **important national interests**, military forces should only be used if they are likely to accomplish their objectives, the costs and risks of their employment are commensurate with the interests at stake, and other non-military means are incapable of achieving our objectives. Such uses of military forces should be selective and limited, reflecting the importance of the interests at stake. We act in concert with the international community whenever possible, but do not hesitate to act unilaterally when necessary.

The decision to employ military forces to support our **humanitarian and other interests** focuses on the unique capabilities and resources the military can bring to bear, rather than on its combat power. Generally, the military is not the best tool for humanitarian concerns, but under certain conditions use of our Armed Forces may be appropriate. Those conditions exist when the scale of a humanitarian catastrophe dwarfs the ability of civilian relief agencies to respond, when the need for relief is urgent and only the military has the ability to provide an immediate response, when the military is needed to establish the preconditions necessary for effective application of other instruments of national power, when a humanitarian crisis could affect U.S. combat operations, or when a response otherwise requires unique military resources. Such efforts by the United States, preferably in conjunction with other members of the international community, will be limited in duration, have a clearly defined mission and end state, entail minimal risk to U.S. lives, and be designed to give the affected country the opportunity to restore its own basic services.

In all cases, the costs and risks of U.S. military involvement must be commensurate with the interests at stake. We will be more inclined to act where there is reason to believe that our action will bring lasting improvement. Our involvement will be more circumscribed when regional states or organizations are better positioned to act than we are. Even in these cases, however, the United States will be actively engaged with appropriate diplomatic, economic, and military tools.

In every case, we will consider several critical questions before committing military force: have we explored or exhausted non-military means that offer a reasonable chance of achieving our goals? Is there a clearly defined, achievable mission? What is the threat environment and what risks will our forces face? What level of effort will be needed to achieve our goals? What is the potential cost -- human and financial -- of the operation? What is the opportunity cost in terms of maintaining our capability to respond to higher-priority contingencies? Do we have milestones and a desired end state to guide a decision on terminating the mission? Is there an interagency or multinational political-military plan to ensure that hard-won achievements are sustained and continued in the mission area after the withdrawal of U.S. forces?

Having decided that use of military forces is appropriate, the decision on how they will be employed is based on two guidelines. First, our forces will have a clear mission and the means to achieve their objectives decisively. Second, as much as possible, we will seek the support and participation of our allies, friends, and relevant international institutions. When our vital interests are at stake, we are prepared to act alone. But in most situations, working with other nations increases the effectiveness of each nation's actions and lessens everyone's burden.

Sustaining our engagement abroad over the long term will require the support of the American people and the Congress to bear the costs of defending U.S. interests -- including the risk of losing U.S. lives. Some decisions to engage abroad with our military forces could well face popular opposition, but must ultimately be judged by whether they advance the interests of our nation in the long run. When we judge it to be in our interest to intervene, we must remain clear in our purposes and resolute in our actions. We must also ensure that protection of that force is a critical priority and that our protection efforts visibly dissuade potential adversaries.

Preparing for an Uncertain Future

We must prepare for an uncertain future, even as we address today's security problems. We need to look closely at our national security apparatus to ensure its effectiveness by adapting its institutions to meet new challenges. This means we must transform our capabilities and organizations -- diplomatic, defense, intelligence, law enforcement, and economic -- to act swiftly and to anticipate new opportunities and threats in today's continually evolving, highly complex international security environment. We must also have a strong, competitive, technologically superior, innovative, and responsive industrial and research and development base and a national transportation system with the resources and capacity to support disaster response and recovery efforts if national mobilization is required.

Strategically, our transformation within the military requires integrating activities in six areas: service concept development and experimentation; joint concept development and experimentation; robust processes to implement changes in the Services and joint community; focused science and technology efforts; international transformation activities; and new approaches to personnel development that foster a culture of bold innovation and dynamic leadership.

The military's transformation requires striking a balance among three critical funding priorities: maintaining the ability of our forces to shape and respond today; modernizing to protect the long-term readiness of the force; and exploiting the revolution in military affairs to ensure we maintain our unparalleled capabilities to shape and respond effectively in the future. Transformation also means taking prudent steps to position us to effectively counter unlikely but significant future threats -- particularly asymmetric threats.

Investment in research and development is an essential element of our transformation effort. It permits us to do what we do best: innovate, not copy. Revolutionary, not evolutionary, leaps will happen in an economy where new ideas can be pursued and quickly translated from vision to reality. It is a competitive advantage that leverages our technological breakthroughs into sustained military superiority. This requires support not only for bringing promising technologies out of the labs for insertion in weapons platforms, but also for fundamental research that will produce the as-yet-unknown technologies that will give the United States the revolutionary advantages we will need in the future. Ultimately, our development efforts must be practical and founded in war-fighting objectives tested through aggressive experimentation.

At the same time we push technological frontiers and transform our military, we also must address future interoperability with multinational partners. Since they will have varying levels of technology, a tailored approach to interoperability that accommodates a wide range of needs and capabilities is necessary. We must encourage our more technically advanced friends and allies to build the capabilities that are particularly important for interoperability, including the command, control, and communication capabilities that form the backbone of combined operations. We must help them bridge technological gaps, supporting international defense cooperation and multinational ventures where they enhance our mutual support and interoperability.

In May 2000, the United States spearheaded a Defense Trade Security Initiative (DTSI); a package of 17 measures designed to enhance allied interoperability and coalition warfighting capabilities by facilitating the transfer of critical U.S.-origin defense items to our allies. At the same time, DTSI promotes a strong and robust allied transnational defense industrial base that can provide innovative and affordable products needed to meet allied warfighting requirements for the 21st century.

Transformation extends well beyond the acquisition of new military systems -- we seek to leverage advanced technological, doctrinal, operational and organizational innovations both within government and in the commercial sector to give U.S. forces greater capabilities and flexibility. Joint Forces Command and the Armed Services are pursuing an aggressive, wide-ranging innovation and experimentation program to achieve that transformation. The Service programs focus on their core competencies and are organized to explore capability improvements in the near-, mid-, and far-term. The Joint Forces Command program ensures a strong joint perspective while also complementing efforts by the Services. A multilateral program has also been developed. NATO's Defense Capabilities Initiative now includes both a NATO-centered and nation-centered concept development and experimentation program, which Joint Forces Command complements with a joint experimentation program to include allies, coalition partners and friends. A recently inaugurated interagency process on Contingency Planning offers the promise of improving the coordination among government agencies well before a crisis is at hand.

The on-going integration of the Active and Reserve components into a Total Force is another important element of the transformation. Despite the rapid pace of technological innovation, the human dimension of warfare remains timeless. In this era of multinational operations and complex threats involving ethnic, religious, and cultural strife, regional expertise, language proficiency, and cross-cultural communications skills have never been more important to the U.S. military. We will continue to transform and modernize our forces by recruiting, training, and retaining quality people at all levels of the military and among its civilian personnel who bring broad skills, an innovative spirit, and good judgement to lead dynamic change into the 21st century.

To support the readiness, modernization and transformation of our military forces, we will work with the Congress to enact legislation to implement the Defense Reform Initiative, which will free up resources through a revolution in business affairs. This effort includes competitive sourcing, acquisition reform, transformation of logistics, and elimination of excess infrastructure through two additional rounds of base realignment and closure. The Administration, in partnership with the Congress, will continue to ensure that we maintain the best-trained, best-equipped and best-led military force in the world for the 21st century.

In the area of law enforcement, the United States is already facing criminal threats that are much broader in scope and much more sophisticated than those we have confronted in the past. We must prepare for the law enforcement challenges arising from emerging technology, globalization of trade and finance, and other international dynamics. Our strategy for the future calls for the development of new investigative tools and approaches as well as increased integration of effort among law enforcement agencies at all levels of government, both in the United States and abroad.

We will continue efforts to construct appropriate 21st century national security programs and structures government-wide. We will continue to foster innovative approaches and organizational structures to better protect American lives, property and interests at home and abroad.

Promoting Prosperity

Globalization, which has drawn our economic and security interests closely together, is an inexorable trend in the post-Cold War international system. It is logical, then, for the United States to capture its positive energy and to limit its negative outcomes, where they exist. In doing both we will be able to promote shared prosperity, the second core objective of our national security strategy.

Strengthening Financial Coordination

As a result of economic globalization, prosperity for the United States and others is inextricably linked to foreign economic developments. Interdependence of this degree makes it incumbent upon the United States to be a cooperative leader and partner in the global financial system. This means doing our part to provide economic and political support to international financial institutions; working to reform them; equipping them with the tools necessary to react to future financial crises; and expanding them to embrace sustainable development efforts in emerging market economies.

Our objective is to build a stable, resilient global financial system that promotes strong global economic growth while providing broad benefits in all countries. Throughout the past seven years, Congress and the President have worked together to enhance funding for international economic institutions and programs. Promoting our prosperity requires us to sustain these commitments in the years and decades ahead.

Drawing on the lessons of the Mexican peso crisis in 1994 and the Asian crises in 1997 and 1998, the United States took the lead in advocating steps to strengthen the architecture of the international financial system so that it more effectively promotes stronger policies in emerging market economies, works to prevent crises, and is better equipped to handle crises when they do occur. As part of a proactive effort to retool the system, the United States proposed creation of the Contingent Credit Line in the IMF to encourage countries to avoid crises. In addition to providing external incentives, it assists these countries to also improve their own debt management. The United States has also taken the initiative in 1999 and 2000, once financial stability was restored, to advocate a series of reforms in the International Monetary Fund (IMF) and the World Bank. These include restructuring lending instruments, introducing greater transparency and accountability into their operations, increasing efforts to reduce vulnerability in advance of crisis, and involving private sector creditors in crisis resolution.

Some developing countries face particularly difficult challenges in their efforts to achieve sustainable development. The HIPC Initiative, as both an international assistance and development tool, provides multilateral debt reduction to countries facing unmanageable debt burdens. In addition to providing $1 billion in support to the HIPC, the United States has led the IMF, World Bank, and other financial institutions to focus attention and resources on the health, education, environment, and poverty issues that surround sustainable development.

Promoting an Open Trading System

In a world where over 96% of the world's consumers live outside the United States, the Nation's domestic economic growth is predicated on our success in expanding trade with other nations.

Since 1993, the President has negotiated over 300 distinct trade agreements. Prominent among these have been the following, which have resulted in declining unemployment, rising standards of living, and robust economic growth in the United States:

> • The North American Free Trade Agreement (NAFTA), which institutionalized our trading relationship with Mexico and Canada. NAFTA created the world's largest free trade zone, expanded trade among its three signatories by over 85%, and generated increased U.S. exports to both Mexico and Canada. Mexico and Canada now take nearly 40% of U.S. exports.

> • The Uruguay Round of the General Agreement on Tariffs and Trade, which created the WTO and created, or substantially expanded, multilateral trade rules and commitments to cover agriculture, services, and intellectual property rights. The WTO has been instrumental in assisting transition economies to progress from centrally planned to market economies and promoting growth and development in poor countries. The United States continuously leads accession negotiations with countries who are seeking WTO membership and who are willing to meet its high standards of market access and rules-based trading.

• Permanent Normal Trade Relations with China, which will provide American farmers, businesses, and industries with market access to the world's most populous nation.

We have consistently advocated trade liberalization with our values in mind, ensuring that increased trade advances, rather than weakens, the rights of workers and the health of the environment.

NAFTA was historic because it mandated environmental and labor protections; it was the first trade agreement to explicitly create the link between trade liberalization and the protection of labor rights and the environment. History was again made this year when the United States entered into a Free Trade Agreement with the Hashemite Kingdom of Jordan. Language in the agreement ensures that liberalization of trade between both nations, the protection of labor rights, and safeguarding the environment are mutually supportive.

The United States ensured that the WTO preamble established environmental protection as an overall objective of the parties to the agreement. In November of 1999, the President issued an executive order on Environmental Reviews of Trade Agreements, an order requiring careful environmental analysis of major new trade agreements. The Office of the United States Trade Representative and the Council on Environmental Quality oversee the implementation of the order, ensuring that promoting trade and protecting the environment go hand-in-hand.

Numerous regional economic partnerships also facilitate global trade. In addition to NAFTA, the Asia Pacific Economic Cooperation Forum (APEC), the President's trade and investment initiative in Africa, the Transatlantic Economic Partnership, and negotiations to create the Free Trade Area of the Americas (FTAA) by 2005 promote open trade in other economic trading regions critical to our national security. With the enactment of the U.S.-Caribbean Basin Trade Partnership Act of 2000 and the Africa Growth and Opportunity Act of 2000, the United States set out to deepen and widen its regional economic relationships.

A Congressional grant of "fast track" authority to the President would enhance his ability to break down foreign trade barriers in a timely manner. "Fast track" promotes American prosperity, just as it expedites domestic job creation and economic growth.

Enhancing American Competitiveness

Gaining the full benefit of more open markets requires an integrated strategy that maintains our technological advantages, promotes American exports abroad, and ensures that export controls intended to protect our national security do not unnecessarily make U.S. high technology companies less competitive globally.

Technological advantage

We will continue to support a vigorous science and technology base that promotes economic growth, creates high-wage jobs, sustains a healthy, educated citizenry, and provides the basis for our future military systems. We will continue to foster the open interchange of people and ideas that underpins our scientific and technological enterprise. We will invest in education and training to develop a workplace capable of participating in our rapidly changing economy. And, we will invest in world-class transportation, information, and space infrastructures for the 21st century.

Export Advocacy

The Administration created America's first national export strategy, working with the private sector to reform the way government and business cooperate to expand exports. The Trade Promotion Coordination Committee has been instrumental in improving export promotion efforts, coordinating our export financing, implementing a government-wide advocacy initiative, and updating market information systems and product standards education.

This export strategy is working, and the United States has regained its position as the world's largest exporter. While our strong export performance has supported millions of new, export-related jobs, we must export more in the years ahead if we are to further strengthen our trade balance position and raise living standards with high-wage jobs.

Enhanced Export Control

The United States is a world leader in high technology exports, including satellites, cellular phones, computers, information security, and commercial aircraft. Some of this technology has direct or indirect military applications, or may otherwise be used by states or transnational organizations to threaten our national security. For that reason, the United States Government carefully controls high technology exports by placing appropriate restrictions on the sale of goods and technologies that could impair our security. Imposing these controls recognizes that, in an increasingly competitive global economy, where there are many non-U.S. suppliers, excessive restrictions will not limit the availability of high technology goods. Rather, they serve only to make U.S. high technology companies less competitive globally, thus losing market share and becoming less able to produce cutting-edge products for the U.S. military and our allies.

Our current export control policy recognizes that we must balance a variety of factors. On the one hand, our policies must promote and encourage the sale of our most competitive goods abroad, while on the other, they must ensure that technologies that facilitate proliferation of F do not end up in the wrong hands. Our policies therefore promote high technology exports by making dual-use license decisions more transparent, predictable, and timely through a rigorous licensing process administered by the Department of Commerce at the same time that we ensure a thorough review of dual-use applications by the Departments of Defense, State, and Energy. Any agency that disagrees with a proposed export can enter the issue into a dispute resolution process that, if necessary, may ultimately rise to the President for adjudication. As a result, reviews of dual-use licenses are today more thorough than ever before. In the case of munitions exports, we are committed to a policy of responsible restraint in the transfer of conventional arms and technologies. A key goal in the years ahead is to strengthen worldwide controls in this area, while facilitating exports of items that we wish to go to our allies and coalition partners. The DTSI, which we look to enhance our future interoperability with our friends and allies, is one such effort that will streamline U.S. munitions export control processes while also devoting additional resources to increasing the security scrutiny applied to munitions exports. The President's decision to seek agreements with close allies that would permit extension of Canada-like exemptions to the ITAR for low risk exports will significantly enhance U.S. competitiveness while also enhancing export controls.

Encryption is an example of a specific technology that requires careful balance. Export controls on encryption must be a part of an overall policy that balances several important national interests, including promoting secure electronic commerce, protecting privacy rights, supporting public safety and national security interests, and maintaining U.S. industry leadership. After reviewing its encryption policy and consulting with industry, privacy and civil liberties groups, the Administration implemented significant updates to encryption export controls in January 2000 and concluded a second update in October 2000. The new policy continues a balanced approach by streamlining export controls while protecting critical national security interests. U.S. companies now have new opportunities to sell their software and hardware products containing encryption, without limits on key length, to global businesses, commercial organizations and individuals. Most U.S. mass-market software products, previously limited to 56 and 64 bit keys, are approved for export to any end user.

In October 2000, the Administration finished another review of its policy to ensure that it maintains balance while taking into account advances in technology and changes in foreign and domestic markets. The most significant change is that the U.S. encryption industry may now export encryption items and technology license-free to the European Union and among several countries (including major trading partners outside of Western Europe). The update is consistent with recent regulations adopted by the European Union; thus assuring continued competitiveness of U.S. industry in international markets. Other policy provisions implemented to facilitate technological development include streamlined export provisions for beta test software, products that implement short-range wireless encryption technologies, products that enable non-U.S.-sourced products to operate together, and technology for standards development. Post-export reporting is also streamlined to increase the relief to U.S. companies of these requirements. Reporting will no longer be required for products exported by U.S.-owned subsidiaries overseas, or for generally available software pre-loaded on computers or handheld devices. These initiatives will assure the continuing competitiveness of U.S. companies in international markets, consistent with the national interest in areas such as electronic commerce, national security, and support to law enforcement.

Similarly, computer technology is an area where the application of export controls must balance our national security concerns with efforts to promote and strengthen America's competitiveness. It is likely we will continue to face extraordinarily rapid technological changes that demand a regular review of export controls. Maintaining outdated controls on commodity-level computers would hurt U.S. companies without benefiting our national security. For these reasons, in February 2000, the Administration announced reforms to computer export controls; the reforms permit sales of higher-level computer technology to countries friendly to the United States. Export control agencies will also review advances in computer technology on an ongoing basis and provide the President with recommendations for updating computer export controls every six months.

U.S. efforts to stem proliferation cannot be effective without the cooperation of other countries. We have strengthened cooperation through a host of international WMD nonproliferation regimes, and we will continue to actively seek greater transparency in conventional arms transfers. These efforts enlist the world community in the battle against the proliferation of WMD, advanced conventional weapons and sensitive technologies, while at the same time producing a level playing field for U.S. business by ensuring that our competitors face corresponding export controls.

Providing for Energy Security

The United States depends on oil for about 40% of its primary energy needs, and roughly half of our oil needs are met with imports. And although we import less than 15% of the oil exported from the Persian Gulf, our allies in Europe and Asia account for about 80% of those exports. For some years, the United States has been undergoing a fundamental shift away from reliance on Middle East oil. Venezuela is consistently one of our top foreign suppliers, and Africa now supplies 15% of our imported oil. Canada, Mexico, and

Venezuela combined supply almost twice as much oil to the United States as the Arab OPEC countries. The Caspian Basin, with potential oil reserves of 160 billion barrels, also promises to play an increasingly important role in meeting rising world energy demand in coming decades.

Conservation measures and research leading to greater energy efficiency and alternative fuels are a critical element of the U.S. strategy for energy security. Our research must continue to focus on developing highly energy-efficient buildings, appliances, and transportation and industrial systems, shifting them where possible to alternative or renewable fuels, such as hydrogen, fuel cell technology, ethanol, or methanol from biomass.

Conservation and energy research notwithstanding, the United States will continue to have a vital interest in ensuring access to foreign oil sources. We must continue to be mindful of the need for regional stability and security in key producing areas, as well as our ability to use our naval power, if necessary, to ensure our access to, and the free flow of, these resources.

Promoting Sustainable Development

True and lasting social and economic progress must occur in a sustainable fashion, that meets the human and environmental needs for enduring growth. Common but reparable impediments to sustainable development include:

- Lack of education, which shuts people out from participation in technological advance.

- Disease and malnutrition, which stifle productivity.

- Pollution, environmental degradation, and unsustained population growth, the remediation of which is much more costly than pre-emptive action.

- Uncontrolled exploitation of natural resources (e.g., overhunting or overfishing of species for food, overcutting of timber for firewood, overgrazing of grasslands by cattle), which can be serious impediments to sustainable development.

- Unsustainable foreign debt obligations, which encourage currency devaluations and capital flight, and can absorb a substantial share of small economies' resources.

Efforts by the United States to foster sustainable development include:

- Promoting sound development policies that help build the economic and social framework needed to encourage economic growth and poverty reduction and facilitate the effective use of external assistance.

- Debt relief to free up developing countries' resources for meeting the basic needs of their people. The United States led the G-7 in adopting the Cologne Debt Initiative for reducing debts owed them by those of the world's poorest countries committed to sound policies that promote economic growth and poverty reduction. The resulting plan is embodied in the HIPC Initiative.

• Public health assistance consisting of grants, loans, and tax incentives for the prevention and treatment of epidemics such as AIDS, malaria, and tuberculosis, as well as the training of individuals to continue providing public health services.

• Human capacity development assistance for basic education and literacy programs, job skills training, and other programs specifically designed to protect women's health, provide educational opportunity, and promote women's empowerment.

• Leadership in the G-8 and OECD to raise environmental standards for export credit agencies and international financial institutions.

In consonance with our values, when a nation that embraces globalization gets left behind, the United States and other proponents of globalization should reach out a hand. Doing so in a manner that promotes not just development, but sustainable development, enhances regional stability, steadily expands the economic growth on which demand for our exports depends, and honors our values, which encourage us to share our wealth with others and inspire growth for more than just ourselves.

Promoting Democracy and Human Rights

The third goal of our national security strategy is to promote democracy, human rights, and respect for the rule of law. Since the founding of the republic, our actions as a Nation have always been guided by our belief that individuals should control their own destinies: economically, politically, and spiritually. Our core values -- political and economic freedom, respect for human rights, and the rule of law -- support this belief, guiding the conduct of our government at home as well as in its dealings with others outside our borders. Much as John Winthrop set a standard for early colonists that we "be as a city upon a hill," nearly four centuries later we still seek to demonstrate the power of our democratic ideals and values by our example. This does not make us turn inward or isolationist, nor should it be interpreted as a bid for hegemony. Rather, in keeping with our values, we have lent our encouragement, support, and assistance to those nations and peoples that freely desire to achieve the same benefits of liberty. The extraordinary movement of nations away from repressive governance and toward democratic and publicly accountable institutions over the last decade reflects how these ideals, when allowed to be freely shared, can spread widely and rapidly, enhancing the security of all nations. Despite some minor setbacks for a few of the newer democracies in the last several years, the trend continues. Since the success of many of those changes is by no means assured, our strategy must focus on strengthening the commitment and capacity of nations to implement democratic reforms, protect human rights, fight corruption and increase transparency in government. For this reason, we join with other nations in creating the community of democracies. In June 2000, 106 countries meeting in Warsaw, Poland endorsed the Warsaw Declaration laying out criteria for democracy and pledging to help each other remain on the democratic path.

Emerging Democracies

The United States works to strengthen democratic and free market institutions and norms in all countries, particularly those making the transition from closed to open societies. This commitment to see freedom and respect for human rights take hold is not only just, but pragmatic. Our security depends upon the protection and expansion of democracy worldwide, without which repression, corruption and instability could engulf a number of countries and threaten the stability of entire regions.

The sometimes difficult road for new democracies in the 1990's demonstrates that free elections are not enough. Genuine, lasting democracy also requires respect for human rights, including the right to political dissent; freedom of religion and belief; an independent media capable of engaging an informed citizenry; a robust civil society and strong Non-governmental Organization (NGO) structures; the rule of law and an independent judiciary; open and competitive economic structures; mechanisms to safeguard minorities from oppressive rule by the majority; full respect for women's and workers' rights; and civilian control of the military.

The United States is helping consolidate democratic and market reforms in Central and Eastern Europe and the newly independent states of the former Soviet Union. Integrating new democracies in Europe into European political, economic and security organizations, such as NATO, OSCE, the EU, and the Council of Europe, will help lock in and preserve the impressive progress these nations have made in instituting democratic and market-economic reforms. Consolidating advances in democracy and free markets in our own hemisphere remains a high priority. In the Asia Pacific region, economic dynamism is increasingly associated with political modernization, democratic evolution, and the widening of the rule of law. Indonesia's October 1999 election was a significant step toward democracy and we will do our part to help Indonesia continue on that path. In Africa, we are particularly attentive to states, such as South Africa and Nigeria, whose entry into the community of market democracies may influence the future direction of an entire region.

The methods for assisting emerging democracies are as varied as the nations involved. Our public diplomacy programs are designed to share our democratic experience in both government and civil society with the publics in emerging democracies. We must continue leading efforts to mobilize international economic and political resources, as we have with Russia, Ukraine, and other countries in Eastern Europe and Eurasia, and with Southeast Europe. We must take firm action to help counter attempts to reverse democracy, as has happened in Fiji, Haiti, Pakistan, Paraguay, and Peru.

We must help democratizing nations strengthen the pillars of civil society by supporting administration of justice and rule of law programs; promoting the principle of civilian control of the military; and training foreign police and security forces to solve crimes and maintain order without violating the basic human rights of their citizens. And we must seek to improve their market and educational institutions, fight corruption and political discontent by encouraging good governance practices, and encourage a free and independent local media that may promote these principles without fear of reprisal.

Adherence to Universal Human Rights and Democratic Principles

We must sustain our efforts to press for adherence to democratic principles, and respect for basic human rights and the rule of law worldwide, including in countries that continue to defy democratic advances. Working bilaterally and through international institutions, the United States promotes universal adherence to democratic principles and international standards of human rights. Our efforts in the United Nations, the Community of Democracies, and other organizations continue to make these principles the governing standards for acceptable international behavior.

Ethnic conflict represents a great challenge to our values and our security. When it erupts in ethnic cleansing or genocide, ethnic conflict becomes a grave violation of universal human rights. We find it clearly opposed to our national belief that innocent civilians should never be subject to forcible relocation or slaughter because of their religious, ethnic, racial, or tribal heritage. Ethnic conflict can also threaten regional stability and may well give rise to potentially serious national security concerns. When this occurs, the intersection of our values and national interests make it imperative that we take action to prevent -- and whenever possible stop -- outbreaks of mass killing and displacement.

At other times the imperative for action will be much less clear. The United States and other nations cannot respond to every humanitarian crisis in the world. But when the world community has the power to stop genocide and ethnic cleansing, we will work with our allies and partners, and with the United Nations, to mobilize against such violence -- as we did in Bosnia and Kosovo.

Our response will not be the same in every case. Sometimes concerted economic and political pressure, combined with diplomacy, is the best answer. At other times, collective military action is appropriate, feasible, and necessary. The way the international community responds will depend upon the capacity of countries to act, and on their perception of their national interests.

Events in the Bosnia conflict and preceding the 1994 genocide in Rwanda demonstrate the pernicious power of inaccurate and malicious information in conflict-prone situations. This made apparent our need to effectively use our information capabilities to counter misinformation and incitement, prevent and mitigate ethnic conflict, promote independent media organizations and the free flow of information, and support democratic participation. As a result, in the spring of 1999, the President directed that all public diplomacy and international information efforts be coordinated and integrated into our foreign and national security policy-making process.

We will also continue to work -- bilaterally and with international institutions -- to ensure that international human rights principles protect the most vulnerable or traditionally oppressed groups in the world -- women, children, indigenous people, workers, refugees, and other persecuted persons. To this end, we will seek to strengthen international mechanisms that promote human rights and address violations of international humanitarian law, such as the LIN Commission on Human Rights and the international war crimes tribunals for the former Yugoslavia and Rwanda. We strongly support wide ratification of the ILO Convention on the Worst Forms of Child Labor. We also aim to implement fully those international human rights treaties to which we are a party.

It is our aim to ensure protection for persons fleeing situations of armed conflict or generalized human rights abuses by encouraging governments not to return refugees to countries where they face persecution or torture. We also seek to focus additional attention on the more vulnerable or traditionally oppressed people by spearheading new international initiatives to combat the sexual exploitation of minors, child labor, use of child soldiers, and homelessness among children.

Violence against, and trafficking in, women and children are international problems with national implications. We have seen cases of trafficking in the United States for purposes of forced prostitution, sweatshop labor, and domestic servitude. Our efforts have expanded to combat this problem, both nationally and internationally, by increasing awareness, focusing on prevention, providing victim assistance and protection, and enhancing law enforcement. The President continues to call upon the Senate to give its advice and consent to ratification to the Convention on the Elimination of all Forms of Discrimination Against Women, which will enhance our efforts to combat violence against women, reform unfair inheritance and property rights, and strengthen women's access to fair employment and economic opportunity.

Promotion of religious freedom is one of the highest concerns in our foreign policy. Freedom of thought, conscience and religion is a bedrock issue for the American people. To that end, the President signed the International Religious Freedom Act of 1998, which provides the flexibility needed to advance religious freedom and to counter religious persecution. In September 1999, we completed the first phase outlined in the Act with publication of the first annual report on the status of religious freedom worldwide, a 1,100 page document covering the status of religious freedom in 194 countries. In October, we designated and sanctioned the Taliban regime in Afghanistan, Burma, China, Iran, Iraq, Sudan, and the Milosevic regime in Serbia as "countries of particular concern" for having engaged in or tolerated particularly severe violations of religious freedom. The United States is active throughout the world assisting those who are persecuted because of their religion and promoting freedom of religious belief and practice. We will continue to work with individual nations and with international institutions to combat religious persecution and promote religious freedom.

The United States will continue to speak out against human rights abuses and it will continue to carry on human rights dialogues with countries willing to engage us constructively. Because police and internal security services can be a source of human rights violations, we use training and contacts between U.S. law enforcement and their foreign counterparts to help address these problems. We do not provide training to police or military units implicated in human rights abuses. When appropriate, we are prepared to take strong measures against human rights violators. These include economic sanctions, visa restrictions, and restricting sales of arms and police equipment that may be used to commit human rights abuses. The Administration proposed legislation to prevent the United States from becoming a safe haven for human rights violators. Both the Immigration and Naturalization Service and the Federal Bureau of Investigation are coordinating investigative efforts on cases involving allegations of human rights abuse to pursue criminal prosecution or administrative removal proceedings in appropriate instances.

In the 1990s, the United States took the lead in seeking compensation for Holocaust survivors, many of whom are impoverished. Over a million individuals are eligible to apply for benefits under agreements concluded with Germany, Austria, and Switzerland. We must now be certain that these agreements are carried out in a fair and equitable manner, and that steps are taken to complete the work we have commenced in the areas of Holocaust education, the payment of Holocaust era insurance policies, and the restitution of art and other property.

Humanitarian Activities

Our efforts to promote democracy and human rights are complemented by our humanitarian programs, which are designed to alleviate human suffering, address resource and economic crises that could have global implications, and pursue appropriate strategies for economic development.

We also must seek to promote reconciliation in states experiencing civil conflict and to address migration and refugee crises. To this end, the United States will provide appropriate financial support and work with other nations and international bodies, such as the International Committee of the Red Cross and the UN High Commissioner for Refugees. We also will assist efforts to protect the rights of refugees and displaced persons and to address the economic and social root causes of internal displacement and international flight.

Private firms and NGOs that principally address human rights issues or democratic principles often become natural allies in assisting in the relief of humanitarian crises. We frequently find we have natural partners in labor unions, human rights groups, environmental advocates, and chambers of commerce in providing international humanitarian assistance. In providing this often life saving assistance, these private and non-governmental groups visibly demonstrate another aspect of, and complement to, our democratic values -- one of helping others in need. All of these values are thus seen by the individuals and governments helped by these organizations, and they underscore why our support of the humanitarian assistance efforts of private and non-governmental groups is in keeping with our values and objective of promoting democracy and human rights.

Supporting the global movement toward democracy requires a pragmatic, long-term effort focused on both values and institutions. Our goal is a broadening of the community of free-market democracies, and stronger institutions and international non-governmental movements committed to human rights and democratization.

III. Integrated Regional Approaches

Our policies toward different regions reflect our overall strategy and guiding principles but must be tailored to the unique challenges and opportunities of each region. Thus, each uses a different application of the elements of engagement and does so in differing degrees. Each region may have its own focused strategic objectives, but, in the end, enhancing our own and the region's security while promoting prosperity, democracy, and human rights are still the ultimate goals.

Europe and Eurasia

European stability is vital to our own security. The United States has three strategic goals in Europe: integration of the region, a cooperative transatlantic relationship with Europe on global issues, and fostering opportunities while minimizing proliferation risks posed by collapse of the Soviet Union. The first goal, building a Europe that is truly integrated, democratic, prosperous, and at peace, would realize a vision the United States launched more than 50 years ago with the Marshall Plan and NATO. The greatest challenge to that remains the integration of Southeastern Europe into the rest of Europe, a strategic objective the United States shares with its NATO allies and the EU. The United States, its allies, and the EU recognize that continued instability, ethnic conflict, and potentially open warfare in Southeastern Europe would adversely affect European security and set back the process of creating a Europe that is truly whole and free. Accordingly, our strategy involves a series of interlocking building blocks, the progressive and interactive implementation of which will achieve step-by-step shared objectives. The building blocks identified below define our common priorities for Southeastern Europe, and -- more importantly -- the pursuit of each helps the attainment of all:

• Coexistence among ethnic groups and the rebuilding of civic society;

• Promotion of the return of refugees and displaced persons to their homes to undo the pernicious consequences of ethnic cleansing;

• Economic reform and revitalization, leading to sustainable economic growth;

• Democratic government based on the rule of law and full respect for human rights;

• Support for the nascent democratic government in the Federal Republic of Yugoslavia (FRY) as a means for advancing its return to the international community;

• A peaceful resolution of the status of Montenegro and Kosovo through arrangements acceptable to all sides;

• Strengthening regional cooperation as a basis for the region's revitalization and eventual integration with the rest of Europe;

• Adherence to international agreements such as the Dayton Accords, especially in recognition of international boundaries.

We are making progress towards our objectives. With the toppling of the Milosevic regime and the ascension of President Kostunica and his government, the process of transition from authoritarian rule to democratic governance is underway in the FRY. The United States and the international community support democratization and economic reform in the FRY to ensure long-lasting change, the removal of impediments to positive social, political, and economic change, and the stability and growth of the entire region of Southeastern Europe. Democratic consolidation and Western integration of the FRY will not be easy, but the United States stands ready to contribute to the achievement of these long-awaited goals.

Elsewhere in Southeastern Europe, elections in Croatia this year saw the victory of a pro-Western, pro-reform government that has become a constructive and stabilizing force in the region. Reform-minded leaders in Macedonia, Albania, and Slovenia continue to press forward with difficult economic reforms. Croatia and Albania both became WTO members this year, on the basis of commercially meaningful commitments that bolster their economic reform programs. Moderate pro-Dayton elements share political power in Bosnia. Kosovars had the opportunity to choose local leaders for the first time this year in Kosovo's democratic elections, and relatively moderate candidates were elected by large majorities. The FRY's new democratic leadership is moving quickly to integrate their nation into Europe and restore constructive cooperation with its neighbors. But much work remains. Economic and political reforms that will allow Southeastern European nations to move forward towards European integration must be accelerated. While Milosevic is out of power in the FRY, democratic change has not yet been consolidated and the new government faces a difficult winter. Greater ethnic reconciliation in Bosnia and Kosovo remains elusive. Security conditions allowing eventual withdrawal of U.S. troops from the region have still not been fully realized. Without a broad strategy of engagement and strong U.S. leadership, our vision of a stable, democratic, and prosperous Europe will not be realized.

Our second goal is to work with our allies and partners across the Atlantic to meet the global challenges no nation can meet alone. This means working together to consolidate this region's historic transition in favor of democracy and free markets; supporting peace efforts in troubled areas both within and outside the region; tackling global threats such as the potential use and continued proliferation of NBC weapons, terrorism, drug trafficking, international organized crime, environmental, problems, or health crises; mass uncontrolled migration of refugees, and building a more open world economy without barriers to transatlantic trade and investment.

Our third goal is to develop the opportunities opened by the collapse of the Soviet Union while minimizing the associated proliferation risks. Russia, Ukraine, and the other New Independent States (NIS) today are undergoing fundamental changes to their political, economic, and social systems -- the outcome will have a profound impact on our own future and security. Core U S. security interests are being advanced through our engagement with these countries, such as through U.S. efforts to help secure and dismantle the former Soviet arsenal of weapons of mass destruction. Our engagement also helps frame the key choices that only the peoples of the former Soviet Union and their leaders can make about their future, their role in world affairs, and the shape of their domestic political and economic institutions. Our strategy utilizes a long-term vision for the region, recognizing that this unprecedented period of transition will take decades, if not generations to complete.

Enhancing Security

NATO remains the anchor of U.S. engagement in European security matters, the foundation for assuring collective defense of Alliance members, and the linchpin of transatlantic security. As the leading guarantor of European security and a force for European stability, NATO must play a leading role in promoting a more integrated and secure Europe; one prepared to respond to new challenges. At the same time, the United States actively supports the efforts of our European partners to develop their own European Security and Defense Policy (ESDP). We further support European efforts to increase and improve capabilities for collective defense and crisis response operations, including the capability to act militarily under the EU when NATO, as a whole, is not engaged. We seek a relationship that will benefit current, and the potential future, members of both organizations, and we intend to remain fully engaged in European security issues, both politically and militarily. The United States has maintained approximately 100,000 military personnel in Europe to fulfill our commitments to NATO. They provide a visible deterrent against aggression and coercion, contribute to regional stability, respond to crises, sustain our vital transatlantic ties, and preserve U.S. leadership in NATO.

NATO is pursuing several initiatives to enhance its ability to respond to the new challenges it will face in the 21st century. At NATO's Fiftieth Anniversary Summit in April 1999, Alliance leaders adopted an expansive agenda to adapt and prepare NATO for current and future challenges. This included an updated Strategic Concept, which envisions a larger, more capable and more flexible Alliance, committed to collective defense and able to undertake new missions. The Defense Capabilities Initiative (DCI) aims to improve defense capabilities and interoperability among NATO military forces, thus bolstering the effectiveness of multinational operations across the full spectrum of Alliance missions, to include Partner forces where appropriate. NATO and the EU are also forging a strategic partnership that will further reinforce European capabilities and contributions to transatlantic security. NATO's WMD Initiative, the other activities of NATO's senior groups on proliferation, and U.S. bilateral NBC defense cooperation with key allies, will increase the ability of the Alliance to counter the threat of NBC weapons and their means of delivery.

NATO enlargement has been a crucial element of the U.S. and Allied strategy to build an undivided, peaceful Europe. At the April 1999 NATO Summit, the alliance welcomed the entry of Poland, Hungary and the Czech Republic as new members. The accession of these three nations has made the Alliance stronger and has reinforced Europe's zone of democratic stability.

Together with our allies, we are pursuing efforts to help other countries that aspire to membership become the best possible candidates. These efforts include the NATO Membership Action Plan and the Partnership for Peace. We are also continuing bilateral programs to advance this agenda, such as the President's Warsaw Initiative, which is playing a critical role in promoting Western-style reform of the armed forces of Central and Eastern Europe, and Eurasia and helping them become more interoperable with NATO. Some European nations do not desire NATO membership, but do desire strengthened ties with the Alliance. The Partnership for Peace provides an ideal vehicle for such relationships. It formalizes relations, provides a mechanism for mutual beneficial interaction, and establishes a sound basis for combined action, should that be desired. This can be seen in the major contributions some Partnership for Peace members have made to NATO missions in the Balkans. Also, on a bilateral basis, the United States has concluded security of classified information agreements with all former Warsaw Pact countries.

NATO is pursuing several other initiatives to enhance its ability to respond to new challenges and deepen ties between the Alliance and Partner countries. NATO's Euro-Atlantic Partnership Council continues to strengthen political dialogue and practical cooperation with all partners, and the Alliance values its distinctive partnership with Ukraine, which provides a framework for enhanced relations and practical cooperation. We welcome Russia's re-engagement with NATO and Permanent Joint Council on the basis of the 1997 NATO-Russia Founding Act. Our shared goal remains to deepen and expand constructive Russian participation in the European security system.

The Organization for Security and Cooperation in Europe (OSCE) has a key role to play in enhancing Europe's stability. It provides the United States with a venue for developing Europe's security architecture in a manner that complements our NATO strategy. In many instances, cooperating through the OSCE to secure peace, deter aggression, and prevent, defuse and manage crises, broadens international support for the resolution of a particular security issue, and gives regional actors greater latitude to develop their own stability mechanisms. The Charter also recognizes that European security in the 21st century increasingly depends on building security within societies as well as security between states. In Istanbul, President Clinton joined the other 29 parties to the Treaty on Conventional Armed Forces in Europe (CFE) in signing the CFE Adaptation Agreement, which will replace obsolete bloc-to-bloc force limitations with nationally-based ceilings and provide for enhanced transparency of military forces through increased information and more inspections. The United States will continue to give strong support to the OSCE as our best choice to engage all the countries of Europe, the Caucasus, and Central Asia in an effort to advance democracy, human rights and the rule of law, and to encourage them to support one another when instability, insecurity, and human rights violations threaten peace in the region.

Kosovo - Securing the Peace

On March 24,1999, after repeated attempts at diplomatic solutions had failed, NATO intervened militarily to end a vicious campaign of ethnic cleansing launched by the Milosevic regime in Belgrade against the ethnic Albanian community in Kosovo. During the eleven-week air campaign that comprised Operation Allied Force, fourteen of the Alliance's nineteen members participated in more than 38,000 combat sorties, almost one third the number flown during the 1991 Desert Storm campaign. In the end, due to the application of force in concert with continued international pressure, Milosevic capitulated, agreeing to NATO's conditions including the return of all refugees, the withdrawal of his military and police forces, and the deployment of an international civil and military presence. This unprecedented display of alliance solidarity ended Belgrade's reign of terror and prevented the real risk that violence in Kosovo would create turmoil throughout the region, undermining its new, fragile democracies and reversing our progress in Bosnia and Herzegovina. NATO's intervention also set the conditions for creating a stable, peaceful, and democratic way of life in Kosovo.

Today, assisting the international community to accomplish those objectives is a NATO-led force (KFOR) of approximately 40,000 personnel from nearly 35 countries (including 6,000 Americans) who continue to protect the peace achieved by last year's military action. The United States never commits its military forces lightly; the decision to contribute to KFOR was firmly grounded in the assessment that national interests, in particular European security and stability, were at stake. At the same time, compared to IFOR and SFOR, we were able to share more of the burden with our European allies, with U.S. troops comprising only 15% of the NATO-led force.

The international community continues to assist refugees and displaced persons to return to their homes and communities, a critical step to social renewal. To date, more than

898,000 Kosovars from diverse ethnic backgrounds have returned (many with the help of KFOR).

Rebuilding infrastructure and promoting economic growth is critical to the hope that one day Kosovo will have a sustainable free market economy. To this end, more than 36,000 new homes have been constructed and more than 70% of private enterprises have been restarted since the end of the war. Much more remains to be done, but the list of impressive economic achievements continues to grow. Supporting democratic institutions and processes is crucial component of our strategy. In October 2000, free and open municipal elections were held for the first time in Kosovo's history, a key step in establishing the autonomous institutions necessary for the Kosovars to govern themselves.

Finally, we continue to promote multiethnic reconciliation in recognition that real democracy requires peaceful coexistence among all ethnic groups and credible protection for minority rights. Statistics indicate a dramatic decline in crime over the past year in Kosovo; however, sporadic ethnic violence still challenges the international community and requires our vigilance.

Today, Kosovo is largely an international protectorate focused on rebuilding itself and inculcating respect for the rule of law. As these intermediate goals are attained, however, Kosovo will continue its journey toward becoming a self-administering democratic community within a unified Europe. Kosovo's final status will ultimately be determined through a political process. The United States will work closely with the EU to ensure that the necessary political and economic environment exists to allow Kosovo's final status to be resolved eventually.

Federal Republic of Yugoslavia (Serbia and Montenegro) - Promoting Democracy

The prospects for sustained peace, stability, and growth throughout the region have improved with the removal of President Milosevic and the election of FRY President Kostunica. President Kostunica's victory signaled the end of destructive and isolationist policies of the Milosevic regime. His government has indicated a desire to seek a future with Europe. The United States remains committed to the people of Serbia and we will support the new democratic governments stated aspirations to reintegrate into Europe and the international community, and to use the transition as an opportunity to foster democracy and market reform in the FRY.

In Montenegro, the democratically elected government of President Djukanovic has made significant progress in implementing political and economic reforms. The United States will continue to support Montenegro and encourage dialogue and negotiation between Montenegro and the new democratic government in Belgrade.

In cooperation with our allies and the international community, efforts are underway to reintegrate the FRY into regional and international organizations. For example, in October 2000, the United States supported FRY admission into the Stability Pact and the United Nations. In November 2000, the U.S. supported the FRY's entry into OSCE. The FRY has also begun discussions with the IMF and World Bank on membership -- as one of the successor states to the Socialist Federal Republic of Yugoslavia -- and has asked to join the European Bank for Reconstruction and Development (EBRD). To bolster the FRY's democratic transition, the United States supported removal of the energy embargo and the travel ban, while maintaining sanctions on financial transactions and trade that could still benefit Milosevic and his cronies. The United States is assessing Serbia's immediate and long-term assistance and humanitarian needs, and is promoting dialogue and negotiation between Montenegro, Kosovo and a new democratic Serb government. While the success of the Kostunica government's effort to consolidate power and build democracy is by no means certain, and while peace in the region remains fragile, the United States stands ready to support the Serbian people at this historic moment in their efforts to have the FRY become a productive member of the international community of democracies.

Bosnia - Implementing Dayton

The full implementation of the Dayton Peace Accords is key to developing Bosnia as a stable, peaceful and economically viable state within Southeastern Europe. Dayton implementation will not only foster Bosnia's integration with Europe, but will also provide the conditions for eventual withdrawal of U.S. troops. To that end, we continue to support the return of refugees, implementation of political and economic reforms, the weakening of the nationalist political parties' grip on political and economic power, the strengthening of state institutions, the reform and integration of the Entity Armed Forces, and the apprehension of remaining war criminals.

While Dayton implementation continues to be measured and incremental, we are making progress. Refugee returns have increased significantly in 2000, in part due to a more secure environment established by NATO-led forces and international financial support. The improved security situation has allowed SFOR to reduce the number of troops in Bosnia from IFOR's initial commitment of 60,000 soldiers in 1995 to current levels of 20,800 -- a reduction by roughly two-thirds. Further progress in implementing Dayton will allow for further reduction in our military presence.

Along with the international community, we continue to press Bosnian officials to accelerate efforts to promote the rule of law, fight corruption, institute economic reforms and create stable state institutions, including those associated with the armed forces. Recent elections have seen growing political pluralism among the electorate and the advancement of moderate, pro-Dayton parties. We seek to support these trends.

Bosnia has benefited from dramatic political change in Croatia, where a reform-oriented government was elected earlier this year. Upon taking power, the new government sent Bosnian Croats the unequivocal message that their future was in Bosnia, not Croatia, and that they should support the full implementation of the Dayton Accords. Croatia's new political orientation has led to the rise of moderate forces in the dominant Bosnian Croat political party and has resulted in a significant decline in Croatian support for the Bosnian Croat component of the Federation army, a necessary step for full military integration in the Federation.

Unfortunately, in the Republika Srpska (RS) some hard-line nationalists still resist efforts to implement several Dayton objectives, from refugee returns to the arrest of war criminals. While we have had some success in moving the Dayton process forward, genuine and sustainable change in the Republika Srpska will depend in part on the cooperation of the new government in the FRY. President Kostunica's public support for the Dayton Accords is encouraging, but must be matched by concrete actions to encourage Bosnian Serbs to pursue their future as part of Bosnia and Herzegovina.

Finally, it is imperative to our objectives that remaining Bosnian war criminals are apprehended and sent to The Hague. Consequently, we strongly support the efforts of the International Criminal Tribunal for the former Yugoslavia (ICTY). In 2000, six additional indicted war criminals were transferred to the ICTY, five of whom were detained by SFOR. The ICTY's work in the region has also benefited from the enhanced cooperation offered by the new government in Croatia.

Cyprus and the Aegean

Tensions on Cyprus, Greek-Turkish disagreements in the Aegean, and Turkey's relationship with the EU have serious implications for regional stability and the evolution of European political and security structures. Our goals are to stabilize the region by reducing long-standing Greek-Turkish tensions, pursuing a comprehensive settlement on Cyprus, and supporting Turkey's full integration into European institutions. A democratic, secular, stable, and Western-oriented Turkey is critical to these efforts and has supported broader U.S. efforts to enhance stability in Bosnia, the nations of the former Soviet Union and the Middle East, as well as to contain Iran and Iraq. The President's trip to Turkey and Greece in November 1999 highlighted encouraging signs of progress for reconciliation in the region, including talks on the Cyprus dispute that are being held under the auspices of the UN in New York and Geneva. The EU's historic decision in December 1999 at its Helsinki Summit to grant candidate status to Turkey -- which the United States strongly encouraged -- reinforced the development of Greek-Turkish rapprochement, while encouraging Turkey to expand its democracy and observance of human rights for all its citizens.

The Baltic States

The special nature of our relationship with Estonia, Latvia, and Lithuania is recognized in the 1998 Charter of Partnership, which clarifies the principles upon which U.S. relations with the Baltic States are based and provides a framework for strengthening ties and pursuing common goals. These goals include integration of Latvia, Lithuania, and Estonia into the transatlantic community and development of close, cooperative relationships among all the states in Northeastern Europe. Through the Northern European Initiative we seek to strengthen regional cooperation, enhance regional security and stability, and promote the growth of Western institutions, trade and investment by bringing together the governments and private sector interests in the Baltic and Nordic countries, Poland, Germany, and Russia.

Northern Ireland

Historic progress was achieved in implementing the Good Friday Accord when, on December 2, 1999, an inclusive power-sharing government was formed in Northern Ireland, the principle of consent was accepted with respect to any change in the territorial status of Northern Ireland, new institutions were launched for North-South cooperation on the island of Ireland, and the Irish Republican Army named a representative to the Independent International Commission on Decommissioning (IICD) of paramilitary weapons (loyalist paramilitaries named their representatives to the IICD soon thereafter). Although differences over the arms decommissioning issue led to suspension of the new institutions on February 11, 2000, the institutions were restored on May 27 following agreement between the British and Irish governments and political leaders. On June 25, the IICD reported that international inspectors visited several IRA arms dumps and concluded that the weapons were secure and could not be used without the IICD becoming aware that this happened. The IRA announced on June 26 that it had reestablished contact with the IICD. These developments followed continued progress in promoting human rights and equality in Northern Ireland, including the introduction of legislation to implement the important recommendations put forward for police reform in the Patten Report issued on September 9, 1999. Disagreements over progress on decommissioning of arms have affected progress.

The United States continues to work with the British and Irish governments and the political leaders in Northern Ireland to achieve full implementation of the Good Friday Accord. Working through the International Fund for Ireland and the private sector, we will help the people seize the opportunities that peace will bring to attract new investment and bridge the community divide, create new factories, workplaces, and jobs, and establish new centers of learning for the 21st century.

Russia and the Newly Independent States (NIS)

There is no historical precedent for the transition underway in Russia, Ukraine, and other NIS. The United States has core national interests at stake in those endeavors and has acted quickly to help people across the NIS to break the back of the Communist system. But the USSR's collapse created new challenges. In Russia, for example, rigidity often gave way to laxness and disorder -- too many rules were replaced by too few. The United States' engagement with each of the NIS recognizes that their transformation will be a long-term endeavor, with far-reaching implications for regional and global stability, as well as disappointments and setbacks along the way.

Open elections are now commonplace in Russia, Ukraine, and most other NIS. We will continue to engage with all these countries to improve their electoral processes and help strengthen civil society by working with grassroots organization, independent media, and emerging entrepreneurs. Though the transition from communism to market democracy is far from complete, the NIS have reduced state controls over their economies and instituted basic protections for private property. It is in our national interest to help them develop the laws, institutions, and skills needed for a market democracy, to fight crime and corruption, and to advance human rights and the rule of law. The conflict in Chechnya represents a major problem in Russia's post-Communist development and relationship with the international community; the means Russia is using in Chechnya are undermining its legitimate objective of upholding its territorial integrity and protecting citizens from terrorism and lawlessness.

The United States strategy toward Russia and the NIS has made every American safer. Threat reduction programs have assisted in the deactivation of former Soviet nuclear warheads and greatly decreased the possibility of sensitive materials, technology, expertise, or equipment falling into the wrong hands. We are working aggressively to strengthen export controls in Russia and the other NIS and to stem proliferation of sensitive missile and nuclear technology, as well as other WMD or advanced conventional weapons to potential regional aggressors such as Iran. The Administration has supported the sovereignty and territorial integrity of the NIS, including through agreement on the adapted CFE Treaty, which was made possible by agreed schedules for the withdrawal of Russian forces from Georgia and Moldova. The integration of Russia, Ukraine, and other NIS with the new Europe and the international community remains a key priority. Despite disagreements over NATO enlargement and the Kosovo conflict, Russian troops serve shoulder-to-shoulder with U.S. and NATO forces in Kosovo and Bosnia. The United States remains committed to further development of the NATO-Russia relationship and the NATO-Ukraine distinctive partnership.

Our engagement with Russia, Ukraine, and other NIS is broad-based and draws upon new ties and partnerships between U.S. and NIS cities, regions, universities, scientists, students, and business people. United States assistance programs have helped these countries begin to develop the laws and legal infrastructure necessary for the rule of law as well as the building blocks of civil society. Still, the challenges ahead in each of these areas are immense. Economic hardship, social dislocation, and rampant crime and corruption threaten the foundations of democratic and law-based governance. Looming environmental problems will complicate NIS governments' ability to develop appropriate and effective responses and policies. Similarly, government pressure on independent media, citizens groups, nongovernmental organizations (NGOs), and religious groups remain a recurring source of concern.

We must continue our efforts to encourage strong and effective property laws and practices in central and Eastern Europe. Such laws are a necessity for a society based on the rule of law, and are a prerequisite for competing in international markets and participating in Western institutions. A starting point is the enactment and enforcement of laws providing for the restitution of property, seized during the Nazi and communist eras, to rightful owners.

Promoting Prosperity

Europe is a key partner in America's global commercial engagement. Europe and the United States produce almost half of all global goods and services; more than 60% of total U.S. investment abroad is in Europe; commerce between us exceeds $1 billion every day; and fourteen million workers on both sides of the Atlantic earn their livelihoods from transatlantic commerce. As part of the New Transatlantic Agenda launched in 1995, the United States and the EU agreed to take concrete steps to reduce barriers to trade and investment through creation of an open New Transatlantic Marketplace and through Mutual Recognition Agreements in goods that eliminate redundant testing and certification requirements. Our governments are also cooperating closely with the civil society dialogues established under the New Transatlantic Agenda: the Transatlantic Business Dialogue, Transatlantic Consumer Dialogue, Transatlantic Environment Dialogue, and Transatlantic Labor Dialogue. These people-to-people dialogues create opportunities for increased communication focusing on best practices, and can help their governments identify and reduce barriers to greater transatlantic interaction. In return, our governments should be committed to listen, learn, and facilitate.

Building on the New Transatlantic Agenda, the United States and the EU launched the Transatlantic Economic Partnership in 1998 to deepen our economic relations, reinforce our political ties and reduce trade frictions. The first element of the initiative is reducing barriers that affect manufacturing, agriculture, and services. In manufacturing, we are focusing on standards and technical barriers that American businesses have identified as the most significant obstacle to expanding trade. In agriculture, we are focusing on regulatory barriers that have inhibited the expansion of agriculture trade, particularly in the biotechnology area. In services, we seek to facilitate trade in specific service sectors, thereby creating new opportunities for the service industries that are already so active in the European market.

The second element of the Transatlantic Economic Partnership is a broader, cooperative approach to addressing a wide range of trade issues. We will continue to refrain from imposing duties on electronic transmissions and develop a work program in the WTO for electronic commerce. We will seek to adopt common positions and effective strategies for accelerating compliance with WTO commitments on intellectual property. We will seek to promote government procurement opportunities, including promoting compatibility of electronic procurement information and government contracting systems. To promote fair competition, we will seek to enhance the compatibility of our procedures with potentially significant reductions in cost for U.S. companies.

The United States strongly supports the process of European integration embodied in the EU. We support EU enlargement, and we are also encouraging bilateral trade and investment in non-EU countries. We recognize that EU nations face significant economic challenges and that periods of economic stagnation have eroded public support for funding outward-looking foreign policies and greater integration. We are working closely with our European partners to expand employment, promote long-term growth, and support the New Transatlantic Agenda.

Within Southeastern Europe, President Clinton and other international leaders launched a relatively new addition to the security architecture of Europe in July 1999. Called the "Stability Pact for Southeastern Europe," the pact is a historic partnership between the international community and the countries of Southeastern Europe, designed to bolster security and advance integration into the European and transatlantic mainstream by accelerating the region's democratic and economic development. By reducing ethnic conflict, promoting democratization and civil society, increasing trade and investment opportunities and supporting regional cooperation, we are promoting stability and prosperity in the region and providing a basis for greater integration into Europe.

Since the inception of the Stability Pact, donors have committed approximately $6 billion in development assistance for the countries of Southeastern Europe. European countries and institutions, together with international financial institutions, are providing over 85% of this assistance. Of this $6 billion, the international community has pledged more than $2.3 billion for over 200 "Quick Start" projects -- many of which are focused on energy, water and transport infrastructure improvements that will have an immediate impact on people's lives. All of the "Quick Start" projects are to be underway by the end of March 2001.

In support of economic development and reform in Southeastern Europe, the U.S. is promoting increased investment throughout the region. OPIC has launched a $150 million equity investment fund that will invest in companies in a range of sectors, including telecommunications, light manufacturing, distribution and consumer goods. The United States and the EBRID have created a $150 million fund to provide technical assistance and lending, in cooperation with local financial institutions, to promote micro, small and medium enterprise development in Southeast Europe. The United States will work with the EBRID to expand the operation of this fund and other activities to Montenegro.

To combat corruption and bureaucratic uncertainty, countries in the region have agreed under the Stability Pact to increase efforts to promote transparency and the rule of law. Under the agreed upon Anti-Corruption Initiative, each member country in the region has committed to make domestic government procurements more transparent, take specific measures to promote public service integrity, and establish a review body to monitor accountability in the administration of foreign aid programs and national anti-corruption efforts.

To promote deeper integration with the rest of Europe and transatlantic institutions, the United States supports EU efforts to play a leading role in the Stability Pact and welcomes closer relations between the EU and the countries of the region. We are urging the EU to strengthen these ties and to act quickly on proposals to open further its markets to Southeastern European products. As the United States' support (in October and November 2000) for FRY admission into the Stability Pact, UN, and OSCE demonstrates, guidelines like those expressed by the Stability Pact serve as worthy benchmarks for inclusiveness into a wider circle of nations.

The United States will continue its strong support for the Stability Pact and broader stabilization efforts. In October 2000, the FRY was formally admitted to join the Stability Pact. The critical challenge for the Stability Pact in the coming months is to persuade the international community and Southeastern Europe that it is in their mutual interests to follow through on important commitments that each has made to the other.

Now that the government in Belgrade has changed, the United States is promoting reintegration of the FRY into regional and international organizations. The energy embargo and travel ban have been lifted, and we are working with the Europeans and other donors to identify priorities for assistance and reconstruction, including Danube River cleanup.

As in other areas in Central and Eastern Europe, as well as the NIS, the United States will continue helping former planned economies integrate into international economic and other institutions and develop healthy business climates. We will continue to promote political and economic reform in Russia, working to create a thriving market economy while guarding against corruption. By supporting historic market reforms in these areas, we help new democracies take root by avoiding conditions, such as corruption and poverty, that can weaken democratic governance and erode the appeal of democratic values.

We are working with many NIS countries to promote their accession to the WTO on commercially fair terms. Building on successful accession of Kyrgyzstan, Latvia, Estonia, Georgia, Albania, Croatia, and Moldova, we have made significant progress on the accession of Armenia and Lithuania. We also have held fruitful discussions on WTO with Russia and Ukraine. We will continue to mobilize the international community to provide assistance to support reform and to help the Central and Eastern European and NIS countries stimulate foreign and domestic private investment. We are also encouraging investment in these countries, especially by U.S. companies.

We focus particular attention on promoting the development of Caspian energy resources and their export to world markets, thereby expanding and diversifying world energy supplies and promoting prosperity in the region.

Getting Caspian energy to world markets will help achieve important goals. It will help enhance prospects for prosperity and independence of the Caspian states. It can help support the development of stable democratic countries, and bolster relationships among the states. Development of Caspian energy resources will improve our energy security, as well as that of Turkey and other allies. It will create commercial opportunities for U.S. companies and other companies around the world. Throughout the region, targeted exchange programs have familiarized key decision makers and opinion molders with the workings of our democracy.

The independence, sovereignty, territorial integrity, and democratic and economic reform of the NIS are important to U.S. interests. To advance these goals, we are utilizing our bilateral relationships and our leadership of international institutions to mobilize governmental and private resources. But the circumstances affecting the smaller countries depend in significant measure on the fate of reform in the largest and most powerful -- Russia. The United States will continue to promote Russian reform and international integration, and to build on the progress that already has been made. Our economic and political support for the Russian government depends on its commitment to internal reform and a responsible foreign policy.

Promoting Democracy and Human Rights

Democratic reforms in Central and Eastern Europe and Eurasia are the best measures to avert conditions that could foster ethnic violence and regional conflict. Already, the prospect of joining or rejoining the Western democratic family through NATO, the EU, and other institutions has strengthened the forces of democracy and reform in many countries of the region and encouraged them to settle long-standing disputes over borders and ethnic minorities. Together with our West European partners we are helping these nations build civil societies.

We continue to promote the integration of Southeastern Europe's democracies into the European mainstream by promoting democratic, economic and military reforms, deepening regional cooperation, and supporting regional efforts to fight organized crime. The opening of a Southeast Europe Cooperation Initiative (SECI) information clearinghouse in Bucharest in the spring of 1999 highlighted efforts by SECI to integrate the efforts of national law enforcement agencies in the fight against cross-border crime. The UN, EU, and NATO operations in the area focused on developing professional civil and military institutions that are respectful and promote human rights and respect for civil authority. Landmark democratic elections in Croatia at the beginning of 2000, and important regional elections, such as those held in Montenegro in June 2000, showed promise for the process of democracy. Where the democratic transition is still in progress, or threatened by external influences, the situation bears continued vigilance. In Kosovo, where violence continued to plague efforts to restore stability, promote tolerance, and begin the establishment of a Kosovar capacity for substantial self-rule, we are determined to succeed in the protection of the rights of individual minorities and the implementation of an ambitious democratic framework for the people of Kosovo.

Municipal elections in Kosovo have paved the way for the establishment of local institutions as the international community encourages the creation of a constitutional framework for Kosovar autonomy called for under the Ramboulliet Agreement and UN Security Council Resolution 1244. As local Kosovars accept responsibility for the process of democracy and protection of minority rights, our efforts in Kosovo will shift from a focus on military security and the training of international and indigenous police forces, to deepened support for those civil efforts that promote democracy, the rule of law, and respect for human rights.

We continue to support the efforts of the International Criminal Tribunal for the former Yugoslavia. In 2000, the pace of detention, transfer, and prosecution of indicted war criminals remained brisk, especially as the new government in Croatia reaffirmed that country's support for the implementation of the Dayton Agreements. New opportunities have also opened with the change of government in Belgrade. We and our European allies have made clear to President Kostunica his obligation to cooperate with the ICTY and our expectation that all indicted war criminals, including former President Milosevic, will be held accountable.

East Asia and the Pacific

Our regional strategy is based on the premise that a stable and prosperous East Asia and Pacific is vital to our own national security interests. United States leadership in expanding mutually beneficial economic relationships and U.S. security commitments within the Pacific rim are central to stability, and even more importantly, they foster an environment within which all Asia/Pacific nations can prosper. We continue to advance this vision of the Asia/Pacific by promoting democracy and human rights, advancing economic integration and rules-based trade, and enhancing security. These three pillars of our security strategy for Asia are mutually reinforcing, and provide the framework for our bilateral and multilateral initiatives. Cooperation with our allies and friends in the region to achieve our common goals remains a cornerstone of our strategy.

Enhancing Security

Our military presence and our strong bilateral security ties have been essential to maintaining the peace and security that have enabled most nations in the Asia-Pacific region to build thriving economies for the benefit of all. To deter aggression and secure our own interests, we maintain about 100,000 military personnel in the region in cooperation with our allies and partners. The U.S.-Japan security alliance anchors the U.S. presence in the Asia-Pacific region. Our continuing security role is further reinforced by our bilateral treaty alliances with the Republic of Korea (ROK), Australia, Thailand and the Philippines. We maintain healthy relations with the Association of Southeast Asian Nations (ASEAN) and support regional dialogue -- such as in the ASEAN Regional Forum (ARF) -- on the full range of common security challenges.

Our security strategy in East Asia and the Pacific encompasses a broad range of potential threats, and includes the following priorities: deterring aggression and promoting peaceful resolution of crises; promoting access to and the security of sea lines of communication in cooperation with our allies and partners; actively promoting our nonproliferation goals and safeguarding nuclear technology; strengthening both active and passive counterproliferation capabilities of key allies; combating the spread of transnational threats, including drug-trafficking, piracy, terrorism and the spread of AIDS; fostering bilateral and multilateral security cooperation, with a particular emphasis on combating transnational threats and enhancing future cooperation in peacekeeping operations; and promoting regional dialogue through bilateral talks and multilateral fora.

Japan

The U.S.-Japan alliance remains the cornerstone for achieving common security objectives and maintaining a peaceful and prosperous environment for the Asia Pacific region. The 1997 revised Guidelines for U.S.-Japan Defense Cooperation create a solid basis for more effective and credible U.S.-Japan cooperation in peacetime, in the event of an armed attack on Japan, and in situations in areas surrounding Japan. They provide a general framework for the roles and missions of the two countries, and facilitate coordination in peacetime and contingencies. The revised Guidelines, like the U.S.-Japan security relationship itself, are not directed against any other country; rather, they enable the U.S.-Japan alliance to continue fostering peace and security throughout the region. In April 1998, in order to support the new Guidelines, both governments agreed to a revised Acquisition and Cross-Servicing Agreement (ACSA) that expands the provision of supplies and services to include reciprocal provision of logistics support during situations surrounding Japan that have an important influence on Japan's peace and security. Japan approved implementing legislation for the Guidelines in the spring of 1999. Japan's generous host-nation support for the U.S. overseas presence also serves as a critical strategic contribution to the alliance and to regional security.

Our bilateral security cooperation has broadened as a result of recent agreements to undertake joint research and development on theater missile defense and to cooperate on Japan's indigenous satellite program. Moreover, we work closely with Japan to promote regional peace and stability, seek universal adherence to the Nuclear Nonproliferation Treaty, and address the dangers posed by transfers of destabilizing conventional arms and sensitive dual-use technologies. Japan is providing $1 billion to the Korean Peninsula Energy Development Organization (KEDO), and consults closely with the United States and ROK on issues relating to North Korea.

Korean Peninsula

Tensions on the Korean Peninsula, albeit reduced as a result of the June 2000 North-South Summit, remain the leading threat to peace and stability in East Asia. The Democratic People's Republic of Korea (DPRK) has publicly stated a preference for peaceful reunification, but continues to dedicate a large portion of its dwindling resources to its huge military forces. Renewed military conflict has been prevented since 1953 by a combination of the Armistice Agreement, which brought an end to open hostilities; the United Nations Command, which has visibly represented the will of the UN Security Council to secure peace; the physical presence of U.S. and ROK troops in the Combined Forces Command, which has demonstrated the alliance's resolve; and, increasingly, diplomatic activities of the United States, ROK, and Japan.

President Kim Dae-jung continues to pursue a course toward peace and stability on the Korean peninsula, seeking new channels of dialogue with North Korea and developing areas of cooperation between South and North. During their June 2000 meeting in Tokyo, President Clinton and President Kim affirmed the importance of the North-South Summit for building a more permanent peace, and the indispensability of the strong U.S.-ROK defense alliance as a stabilizing pillar for the region. The United States is working to create conditions of stability by maintaining solidarity with our South Korean and Japanese allies, emphasizing America's commitment to shaping a peaceful and prosperous Korean Peninsula, and ensuring that a struggling North Korea does not opt for a military solution to its political and economic problems.

Peaceful resolution of the Korean conflict with a democratic, non-nuclear, reunified peninsula will enhance peace and security in the East Asian region and is clearly in our strategic interest. We have taken steps to improve bilateral political and economic ties with North Korea -- consistent with the objectives of our alliance with the ROK -- to draw the North into more normal relations with the region and the rest of the world. Secretary Albright furthered that objective during her historic meeting with North Korean leader Kim Jong 11 in late October 2000. The United States has also outlined to the DPRK what steps it must take to cut all ties to terrorism, and be considered for removal from the list of state sponsors of terrorism. But our willingness to continue to improve bilateral relations will continue to be commensurate with the North's cooperation in efforts to reduce tensions on the peninsula and to stem its NBC weapons programs.

South Korea has set an example for nonproliferation by accepting the 1991 Denuclearization Agreement, agreeing to IAEA safeguards, and developing a peaceful nuclear program that brings benefits to the region. We are firm that North Korea must maintain the freeze on production and reprocessing of fissile material, dismantle its graphite-moderated reactors and related facilities, and fully comply with its NPT obligations under the Agreed Framework. The United States, too, must fulfill its obligations under the Agreed Framework, and the Administration will work with the Congress to ensure the success of our efforts to address the North Korean nuclear threat.

Beyond fully implementing the Agreed Framework, we seek to eliminate North Korea's indigenous and export missile program and their weapons of mass destruction through a step-by-step process. Based on U.S.-North Korean discussions, North Korea has undertaken to refrain from flight testing long-range missiles of any kind as we move toward more normal relations. Working closely with our ROK and Japanese allies, we will improve relations with North Korea on the basis of it moving forward on the missile and WMD agendas, and we will take necessary measures in the other direction if the North chooses to go down a different path.

We encourage the North to work with South Korea to implement the agreements reached at the North-South Summit; continue the United Nations Command-Korean People's Army General Officer Dialogue at Panmunjom; participate constructively in the Four Party Talks among the United States, China, and North and South Korea to reduce tensions and negotiate a peace agreement; and continue our efforts to recover the remains of American servicemen missing since the Korean War.

Pyongyang's more recent diplomatic and economic outreach to the rest of the world are encouraging, but as yet no reciprocal confidence-building measures have been forthcoming. It is crucial that the United States and the ROK maintain deterrence during the process of reconciliation and economic integration on the Korean Peninsula. We favor a step by step process of using reciprocal confidence building measures that link economic and diplomatic initiatives to real reductions in the military threat on the peninsula.

China

A stable, open, prosperous People's Republic of China (PRC) that respects the rule of law and assumes its responsibilities for building a more peaceful world is clearly and profoundly in our interests. The prospects for peace and prosperity in Asia depend heavily on China's role as a responsible member of the international community. Our policy toward China is both principled and pragmatic, expanding our areas of cooperation while dealing forthrightly with our differences.

In recent years, the United States and China have taken a number of steps to strengthen cooperation in international affairs: intensive diplomatic work to restore relations damaged by our mistaken bombing of the Chinese Embassy in Belgrade; successful conclusion of a bilateral agreement on Chinese WTO accession; two presidential bilateral meetings in 2000; regular exchanges of visits by cabinet and sub-cabinet officials to consult on political, military, security, nonproliferation, arms control, economic, financial, and human rights issues; cooperating in efforts to account for Americans missing as a result of World War II and the Korean War; establishing a consultation mechanism to strengthen military maritime safety; holding discussions on humanitarian assistance and disaster relief, and environmental security; and establishing working groups on law enforcement cooperation. China is also a participant in science, technology, and health research. Our cooperation in promoting environmental protection and sustainable development is steadily increasing to the benefit of U.S. interests in the Asia-Pacific region.

At the same time, China's rise as a major power presents an array of potential challenges. Many of China's neighbors are closely monitoring China's growing defense expenditures and modernization of the People's Liberation Army (PLA). Given international and regional focus on China's growing military power, China's adherence to multilateral nonproliferation and arms control regimes, as well as increased military transparency, is of growing importance.

United States interests have been advanced in discussions with China on arms control and nonproliferation issues. We have advanced our dialogue on nonproliferation and arms control through exchanges at the Secretary of Defense, Secretary of State, and sub-cabinet level in 1999 and 2000, building on previous accomplishments. The United States and China announced in earlier exchanges that they will not target their strategic nuclear weapons at each other and confirmed their common goal of halting the spread of WMD. Both our nations have signed the Comprehensive Test Ban Treaty. We have consulted on the Missile Technology Control Regime and missile nonproliferation, and we continue to press China to exercise restraint in its missile policies and practices. In November 2000, China publicly announced that it would reinforce its export control system, and that it had no intention to assist any country in the development of ballistic missiles that could be used to deliver nuclear weapons. Both nations have ratified the Chemical Weapons Convention, and China has further strengthened its controls on the export of dual-use chemicals and related production equipment and technology to assure they are not used for production of chemical weapons. Both nations have called for strengthening of the Biological Weapons Convention and early conclusion of a protocol establishing a practical and effective mechanism to enhance compliance and improve transparency. We also reached agreement with China on practices for end-use visits on U.S. high technology exports to China and we will continue a dialogue on implementation of this agreement.

China is working with the United States on important regional security issues. On the Korean Peninsula, the United States and China share an interest in peace and stability and worked together to support the June 2000 North-South Summit. We have both worked to convince North Korea to freeze its dangerous nuclear program, and believe the four-party peace talks are an important tool in working toward establishment of peace and stability in Northeast Asia.

To help maintain peace, security, and stability in the Western Pacific, and to promote our broad foreign policy objectives, we are implementing fully the terms of the Taiwan Relations Act by maintaining unofficial relations between the American people and the people of Taiwan. We are keeping the focus on peaceful resolution by working assiduously to encourage the PRC and Taiwan to reestablish direct dialogue, while maintaining our firm commitment to Taiwan's self-defense by providing defensive arms to Taiwan.

Our key security objectives for the future include: sustaining the strategic dialogue begun by the recent summits and other high-level exchanges; enhancing stability in the Taiwan Strait by maintaining our "one China" policy, promoting peaceful resolution of cross-Strait issues, and encouraging dialogue between Beijing and Taipei; strengthening China's adherence to international nonproliferation norms, particularly with respect to export controls on ballistic missile and dual-use technologies; encouraging China to adopt broader, more effective export control policies; achieving greater openness and transparency in China's military; encouraging a constructive PRC role in international affairs through active cooperation in multilateral fora such as the ASEAN Regional Forum (ARF) and the Asia Pacific Economic Cooperation Forum (APEC); and improving law enforcement cooperation in such areas as counterterrorism, counternarcotics, and migrant trafficking.

Southeast Asia and the Pacific

Our strategic interest in Southeast Asia centers on developing regional, multilateral, and bilateral security and economic relationships that assist in conflict prevention and resolution. United States security objectives in the region are: strengthening our security alliances and partnerships with Australia, Thailand, the Philippines, and Singapore; sustaining facilities access arrangements with these countries and other ASEAN nations; and encouraging effective multilateral cooperation by expanding participation in regional exercises geared toward disaster relief operations and combating such transnational threats as piracy and drug-trafficking. We continue to view ASEAN as the key regional institution for enhancing security and prosperity. We will continue to work on our relationship with ASEAN and enhance our multilateral security dialogue under the ARF. We must also pursue multilateral, or sometimes bilateral, initiatives with ASEAN to address transnational issues such as the spread of infectious disease, alien smuggling, trafficking in women and children, environmental protection, and combating organized crime, particularly the flow of heroin from Burma and other countries in the region.

Promoting Prosperity

A prosperous and open Asia/Pacific is key to the economic health of the United States. Thirty percent of U.S. exports go to Asia, supporting millions of U.S. jobs, and we export more to Asia than Europe. The economic benefits of a strong Asia/Pacific are likely to increase as China and Taiwan enter into the WTO. Our historic decision to grant Permanent Normal Trade Relations to China will enable U.S. businesses to expand into China under a rules-based trading regime.

Our economic objectives in the region include the following: continuing recovery from the financial crisis; furthering progress within APEC toward liberalizing trade and investment; increasing U.S. exports to Asia/Pacific countries through market-opening measures and leveling the playing field for U.S. business; and concluding the WTO accession negotiations for the PRC and Taiwan on satisfactory commercial terms.

Our strategy to meet these objectives has four key elements: support for economic reforms and market liberalization; working with international financial institutions to provide well-targeted economic and technical assistance in support of economic reforms; providing bilateral humanitarian aid and contingency bilateral financial assistance if needed; and urging strong policy actions by Japan and the other major economic powers to promote global growth.

The United States will continue to work with the IMF, the World Bank, other international financial institutions, the governments in the region, and the private sector to strengthen financial markets, bolster investor confidence, and deepen on-going reforms in the region's economies. In doing so, we will remain mindful of the need to promote protection of worker rights. We will continue to encourage South Korea, Thailand, and Indonesia to implement economic reforms to lay a solid basis for long-term economic growth. U.S. initiatives in APEC will open new opportunities for economic cooperation and permit U.S. companies to expand their involvement in substantial infrastructure planning and construction throughout the region. We will continue our efforts to encourage all Asia Pacific nations to pursue open markets.

China

Integrating the PRC more fully into the global trading system is manifestly in our national interest. China is a major potential market for our goods and services. Our exports to China already support hundreds of thousands of jobs across our country and China's WTO entry will significantly expand that number.

An important part of integrating China into the market-based world economic system is opening China's highly protected market through elimination of trade barriers and removal of distorting restraints on economic activity. We have negotiated and vigorously enforced landmark agreements to combat piracy of intellectual property and advance the interests of our creative industries. We have also negotiated -- and vigorously enforced -- agreements on textile trade. We will continue to press China to open its markets as it engages in sweeping economic reform, and to respect and adhere to core labor standards as codified by the ILO. Most recently, the United States reached a market access agreement with China, paving the way for China's accession to the World Trade Organization. The bilateral agreement concluded in November 1999 will create jobs and opportunities for Americans through the opening of Chinese markets, promote economic reform in China, and enhance the understanding of the Chinese people of the rule of law in the development of their domestic civil society in compliance with international obligations. We are now working with other Working Party members to complete the multilateral negotiation of China's WTO accession. Our enactment of Permanent Normal Trade Relations status for China will accelerate and expand these favorable trends.

Japan

Japan has a crucial role to play in Asia's economic health: generating substantial growth to help maintain a growing world economy and absorb a growing share of imports from emerging markets We have urged Japan to reform its financial sector, stimulate domestic demand, deregulate its economy, and further open its markets to foreign goods and services. The Administration continues to make progress on increasing market access in Asia's largest economy. Since the beginning of the first Clinton Administration, the United States and Japan have reached 39 trade agreements designed to open Japanese markets in such key sectors as autos and auto parts, civil aviation, and insurance. In the Enhanced Initiative on Deregulation, Japan agreed to regulatory reforms to promote domestic demand-led growth and also to increase business opportunities for U.S. firms in such vital areas as telecommunications, competition policy enforcement, and medical/pharmaceutical products. Through the Foreign Direct Investment Initiative, Japan agreed to measures to improve the environment for foreign investment. As a result, U.S. firms are increasing their presence in the Japanese market by acquiring Japanese firms, and are thereby contributing to Japan's economic recovery. The Administration also has intensified efforts to monitor and enforce trade agreements with Japan to ensure that they are fully implemented. The United States also uses multilateral venues, such as WTO dispute settlement and negotiation of new multilateral agreements, to further open markets and accomplish our trade objectives with Japan. The U.S.-Japan Common Agenda is a bilateral U.S.-Japan program coordinating scientific and financial resources of the world's two largest economies on more than seventy projects worldwide. The projects focus on eradicating infectious disease, protecting the environment, and promoting scientific and technological cooperation.

Republic of Korea

The United States will continue its strong support for South Korean efforts to reform its economy, liberalize trade and investment, strengthen the banking system, and implement the IMF program. We will also continue to explore concrete steps to promote growth in both our countries, more fully open our markets, and further integrate the Republic of Korea into the global economy.

Southeast Asia and the Pacific

The United States strongly supports efforts to sustain and strengthen economic recovery in the ten nations of ASEAN. We accomplish this by maintaining our open market for Southeast Asian goods and services as well as our support for IMF-led recovery programs for several ASEAN nations. There are challenges ahead. Thailand's economic recovery is continuing, however, high oil prices and the slow pace of banking and corporate sector reforms are impeding Thailand's full economic recovery from the financial crisis. Thais are preparing for elections in January 2001. The survival and vindication of Thailand's new constitution would reflect well on the future of democracy in Southeast Asia, but the Thais worry about political stability ahead. In Indonesia, slow progress on corporate and financial sector restructuring endangers economic recovery. Rapid sale of assets held by the Indonesian Bank Restructuring Agency (IBRA) is the key to alleviating the large public debt burden and improving investor sentiment. IBRA has begun to move ahead, but without stronger support from the government, progress will remain uneven. Privatization of the banking sector, which has been largely under government control since the crisis, is another area of worrying policy drift. With Vietnam, we are working toward completion of a broad commercial agreement that will open that country's markets, promote economic reform, and open the way for congressional approval of Normal Trade Relations for Vietnam. Nearby in Singapore, in November 2000, President Clinton and Prime Minister Goh of Singapore agreed to launch negotiations for a free trade agreement. In addition to the economic benefits both countries would be expected to gain, the two leaders have recognized the importance of continued U.S. engagement in Asia based on economic and security interests. Working with ASEAN members to address environmental degradation -- from forest fires and haze, to fisheries depletion and deforestation -- while striving for sustainable economic growth, is a high priority.

Australia and New Zealand

We will continue to build on our close working relationship with Australia and New Zealand to strengthen our bilateral trade and economic relationships. We will also work with these two key partners to develop international support for further action by APEC and by the World Trade Organization to develop rules-based trade and encourage sector liberalization.

Promoting Democracy and Human Rights

The United States will continue to support the democratic aspirations of Asian/Pacific peoples and to promote respect for human rights. Our strategy is best served through close coordination with our allies and friends in the region, both at the governmental and non-governmental organization level. Our priorities include: progress on human rights, religious freedom and rule of law issues in China; a meaningful political dialogue between the ruling authorities in Burma and the democratic opposition; supporting Indonesia's democratic transition; and contributing to East Timor's transition to independence.

Indonesia

The United States strongly supports a united, prosperous, and democratic Indonesia that plays a positive role in regional security. The October 1999 election was a historic moment for Indonesia, putting it on course to become the world's third largest democracy. We continue to assist Indonesia in managing the considerable challenges of national reconciliation, democratic reform and economic recovery. We have tailored a comprehensive assistance package focused on: economic development; humanitarian assistance and infrastructure development in strife-torn areas; and technical assistance in key government sectors designed to reinforce the democratic process and the rule of law.

Burma

The United States will continue to work with other concerned states to create the conditions for a meaningful dialogue between the regime and the democratic opposition led by Aung San Suu Kyi. Our strategy includes investment and other sanctions to increase pressure on the regime to respect basic human rights. At the same time, we support the efforts of the United Nations Secretary General to use his good offices to promote dialogue leading to a democratic transition.

East Timor

The UN Transitional Authority in East Timor (UNTAET), established in October 1999, followed on the success of the UN-sanctioned International force in East Timor (INTERFET). The UN-Sanctioned International Force in East Timor was an Australian-led mission that deployed in September 1999, with U.S. support, to quell the post-referendum violence in East Timor. The UN Transitional Authority in East Timor took over security responsibilities from INTERFET in February 2000. UNTAET has continued to further the goal of an independent and viable East Timor. Our contributions have a strong impact on UNTAET's success. We are providing long-term development assistance and transitional employment opportunities to the East Timorese people, as well as financial and technical support for the UN transition administration. Our military forces have provided on-going health and infrastructure support directly to the East Timorese people, and have maintained a presence to coordinate humanitarian and civic assistance projects. We remain committed to attaining a durable solution to the plight of East Timorese refugees in Indonesia. A challenge for the future is assisting with the establishment of a small yet viable East Timor Defense Force.

The Western Hemisphere

Our hemisphere enters the 21st century with an unprecedented opportunity to secure a future of stability and prosperity-building on the fact that virtually all nations in the hemisphere are democratic and committed to free market economies. The end of armed conflict in Central America and other improvements in regional security have coincided with remarkable political and economic progress throughout the Americas. The people of the Americas are taking advantage of the vast opportunities being created as emerging markets are connected through electronic commerce and as maturing democracies allow individuals to more fully express their preferences. Sub-regional political, economic, and security cooperation in North America, the Caribbean, Central America, the Andean region, and the Southern Cone have contributed positively to peace and prosperity throughout the hemisphere. Equally important, the people of the Americas have reaffirmed their commitment to combat together the difficult threats posed by drug trafficking and corruption. The United States, which helped shape this new climate in the hemisphere, seeks to secure its benefits while safeguarding our citizens against these threats.

Enhancing Security

Our strategy of engagement in the Western Hemisphere has included strengthening and expanding U.S. defense cooperation with friends throughout the region, and supporting their efforts to institute democratic norms within their defense establishments including civilian control, transparency, and public accountability. As these democratic norms take root, regional confidence builds. The United States also will continue working to strengthen regional and sub-regional cooperative security mechanisms that could serve to deepen regional confidence and foster sustained regional stability. We will continue to offer our strong support for the peaceful resolution of disputes in the region, and will encourage continued dialogue and peaceful engagement among nations of the region to achieve this goal. While respecting sovereignty concerns, we remain committed to promoting cooperative approaches throughout the hemisphere to international peacekeeping threats and humanitarian crises.

The principal threats to hemispheric stability are transnational in nature, such as drug trafficking, money laundering, illegal immigration, firearms trafficking, and terrorism. In addition, our hemisphere is leading the way in recognizing the dangers to national and regional stability produced by corruption and ineffective judicial systems. All of these produce adverse social effects at home and undermine the sovereignty, democracy, and national security of nations in the hemisphere.

Particularly pernicious is the threat of drug trafficking. Working with the OAS and other organizations, we seek to eliminate the scourge of drug trafficking in our hemisphere. Countries of the hemisphere are striving to better organize and coordinate efforts to extradite and prosecute individuals charged with drug trafficking and related crimes; combat money laundering; seize assets used in criminal activity; halt illicit traffic in precursors and essential chemicals; strike at the financial support networks; enhance national drug abuse awareness and treatment programs; and drastically curtail illicit crops through alternative development and eradication programs. In the Caribbean, and bilaterally with Mexico and Colombia, we are working to increase counterdrug and law enforcement cooperation.

At the same time, we recognize linkages between the threats posed to the United States as the principal consumer of illicit drugs and related threats posed to source countries and transit zone states. Accordingly, as we seek to expand regional cooperation in the counterdrug arena, we recognize our obligation to aggressively combat the illegal export of U.S.-origin weapons to criminal and insurgent groups that are engaged in, or benefit from, drug trafficking.

Colombia is of special importance because drug trafficking is fueling the longest running internal conflict in the region. The combination of armed insurgents, growing paramilitary movement, corruption, and economic malaise extends beyond its borders and has implications for regional peace and security. To turn the tide, the United States is providing the Colombian Government assistance to wage a comprehensive effort to promote the mutually reinforcing goals of peace, illicit drug control, economic development, and respect for human rights. The Government of Colombia has developed a comprehensive six-year strategy, *Plan Colombia, to* revive its economy, strengthen the democratic pillars of society, promote the peace process, and reduce drug production and trafficking. We are providing significant assistance for *Plan Colombia* in a manner that will concurrently promote U.S. and Colombian interests, and we will encourage our allies and international institutions to do the same.

The extent of bilateral cooperation with Mexico in the fight against drug trafficking is unprecedented. We have created the High-Level Contact Group and a variety of working groups to reach a joint diagnosis and settle on a common strategy. Moreover, the mutually agreed upon Performance Measures of Effectiveness will allow us to better evaluate our counterdrug efforts. We are working together to reduce demand for illegal drugs, combat money laundering, avoid the misuse of precursors and essential chemicals, stop the illegal trafficking of arms or migrants, broaden our ability to intercept drugs, and apprehend those who are involved in drug trafficking.

Promoting Prosperity

Economic growth and integration in the Americas will profoundly affect the prosperity of the United States in the 21st century. This begins with our immediate neighbors, Canada and Mexico. Since the 1989 U.S.-Canada Free Trade Agreement, and subsequently the 1993 North American Free Trade Agreement, our trade with Canada and Mexico has grown rapidly. Canada remains our largest trade partner, and Mexico has become our second largest trading partner. The United States and Mexico have also resolved important trade differences, made progress toward easier access for the relevant products of both nations, and consolidated our trade area as one of the most powerful in the world. In the hemisphere as a whole, our trade initiatives offer a historic opportunity to capitalize on and strengthen the unprecedented trend toward democracy and free market economics.

We seek to advance the goal of an integrated hemisphere of free market democracies by building on NAFTA. Formal negotiations are in progress to initiate the Free Trade Area of the Americas (FTAA) by 2005. The negotiations cover a broad range of important issues, including market access, investment, services, government procurement, dispute settlement, agriculture, intellectual property rights, competition policy, subsidies, anti-dumping, and countervailing duties. We will seek to ensure that the agreement also supports workers' rights, environmental protection and sustainable development. To address the concerns of smaller economies prior to completion of the FTAA, and in light of the increased competition NAFTA presents, we have obtained Congressional approval for enhanced trade preferences offered to Central American and Caribbean countries under the Caribbean Basin Trade Partnership Act.

The United States will continue its effective partnership with the IMF, the World Bank, the Inter-American Development Bank, the governments of Latin America, and the private sector to help the region's countries in their transition to integrated, market economies. A key target of this partnership is assisting the reform and recovery of banking sectors hurt by financial market turmoil over the past several years. We will continue to support financial and economic reform efforts in Brazil and Argentina to reduce their vulnerability to external shocks, as well as help Ecuador on its difficult road to economic recovery and sustainable levels of debt service. Similarly, we will continue to play an active role with our regional partners in facilitating timely responses to, and recovery from natural disasters, such as Hurricane Mitch in Honduras and Nicaragua, Hurricane Keith in Belize, and the adverse economic disruptions throughout the region resulting from El Nino.

Helping countries in the hemisphere to translate economic growth into social progress is critical for promoting sustainable growth and sustaining democracy. Despite recent progress, Latin American and Caribbean countries have the greatest income disparities of any region -- with the poorest 20% of individuals receiving just 4.5% of the total income within the region. We will continue to support investments in human development, particularly the provision of stronger and more efficient basic education and health services. Between the United States and Mexico there has been significant growth in educational programs emphasizing literacy, bilingual education and exchanges between classroom teachers, cultural institutions and artists. In the area of health, we are creating the Border Health Commission to study the epidemiology of the border area in order to battle diseases.

We also view it as essential that economic prosperity in our hemisphere be pursued in an environmentally sustainable manner. From our shared seas and freshwater resources to migratory bird species and transboundary air pollution, the environmental policies of our neighbors can have a direct impact on quality of life at home. Working with Mexico, we have taken concerted action to monitor air quality, intensify research on environmental health issues, follow the cross-border movement of toxic wastes or illegal migrants, coordinate activities that will benefit nature preserves, and use debt relief to further protect tropical forests. United States Government assistance to the region recognizes the vital link between sustainable use of natural resources and long-term prosperity, a key to developing prosperous trading partners in this hemisphere.

Promoting Democracy and Human Rights

Latin American nations have made notable advances over the last several years, with the restoration of democratic institutions in old democracies like Chile and Uruguay, the consolidation of democratic practices in countries like Nicaragua and Guatemala, and the move to a competitive democratic system in Mexico where the freest and most transparent presidential and general elections in the country's history were held in July 2000. Of particular significance has been the growing hemispheric consensus on the importance of defending democracy when threatened. Through the OAS, the nations of the Hemisphere have stood firm in support of constitutionally-elected governments under stress, as in the cases of Ecuador, Guatemala, Paraguay, Haiti, and the Dominican Republic. In Peru, the OAS is playing a critical role in facilitating democratic reforms that are expected to lead to free and fair elections in April 2001. We are committed to working with our partners in the region to further consolidate democratic governance and guard against democratic reversals.

But our ability to sustain the hemispheric agenda crafted through the Summit of the Americas process and the OAS depends in part on meeting the challenges posed by weak democratic institutions, persistently high unemployment and crime rates, and serious income disparities. In some Latin American countries, citizens will not fully realize the benefits of political liberalization and economic growth without regulatory, judicial, law enforcement, and educational reforms, as well as increased efforts to integrate all members of society into the formal economy.

The hemisphere's leaders are committed to strengthening democracy, justice, and human rights. They have pledged to intensify efforts to promote democratic reforms at the regional and local level, protect the rights of migrant workers and their families, improve the capabilities and competence of civil and criminal justice systems, and encourage a strong and active civil society. Specific initiatives have included: ratification of the Inter-American Convention Against Corruption to strengthen the integrity of governmental institutions; creation of a Special Rapporteur for Freedom of Expression as part of the Inter-American Commission for Human Rights; and establishment of an Inter-American Justice Studies Center to facilitate training personnel and exchanging information, and other forms of technical cooperation to improve judicial systems.

Education is at the centerpiece of reforms aimed at making democracy work for all the people of the Americas. The Summit Action Plan adopted at Santiago in 1998 seeks to ensure by the year 2010 primary education for 100% of children and access to quality secondary education for at least 75% of young people.

We are also seeking to strengthen norms for defense establishments that are supportive of democracy, transparency, respect for human rights, and civilian control in defense matters. Through continued engagement with regional security forces and civilian personnel, facilitated by establishment of the Center for Hemispheric Defense Studies, our own modest military activities, and presence in the region, we are helping to increase civilian expertise in defense affairs and reinforce the positive trend in civilian control.

The United States supports the full implementation of enduring political, economic, security, and judicial reforms in Haiti. Recognizing the severe challenges that confront the Haitian people, we will continue to provide humanitarian assistance directly to those in need through non-governmental organizations, while working with civil society and Haitian authorities to encourage development of sustainable democratic institutions. In cooperation with the OAS and international financial institutions, we will maintain pressure on the Haitian regime to adopt credible, free, and fair electoral processes and to privatize state-owned industries as an incentive to foreign investment. Concerned by the continued use of Haiti as a transshipment point for illegal drugs entering the United States, we support the further development of the counterdrug capabilities by the Haitian National Police as well as modernization and reform of judicial institutions.

The United States remains committed to promoting a peaceful transition to democracy in Cuba and forestalling a mass exodus that would endanger the lives of migrants and the security of our borders. While maintaining pressure on the regime to make political and economic reforms, we continue to encourage the emergence of a civil society to assist the transition to democracy when the change comes. As the Cuban people feel greater incentives to take charge of their own future, they are more likely to stay at home and build the informal and formal structures that will make transition easier. Meanwhile, we remain firmly committed to bilateral migration accords that ensure migration in a safe, legal, and orderly manner.

The Middle East, North Africa, Southwest, and South Asia

Enhancing Security

The United States has enduring interests in pursuing a just, lasting and comprehensive Middle East peace, ensuring the security and well-being of Israel, helping our Arab partners provide for their security, and maintaining worldwide access to a critical energy source. Our strategy reflects those interests and the unique characteristics of the region as we work to strengthen peace and stability.

The Middle East Peace Process

A historic transformation has taken place in the political landscape of the Middle East over the last five years. Peace agreements have been reached requiring concerted implementation efforts, and new agreements are possible which hold out the hope of ending the conflict between Israel and its Arab neighbors. The United States -- a key sponsor of the peace process -- has a clear national interest in seeing the process deepen and widen. We will continue our steady, determined leadership; standing with those who take risks for peace, standing against those who would destroy it, lending our good offices where we can make a difference, and helping bring the concrete benefits of peace to people's daily lives.

Before the death of Syrian President Assad, Israel and Syria had narrowed their differences to a remarkable degree. Key differences remained, but the broad features of an agreement -- and many of its details -- were well established. The United States remains determined to continue to assist the two sides to find a way to overcome their final differences and hopeful that we will be able to do so. We also continue to believe that progress in Israeli-Syrian negotiations will allow progress on negotiations between Israel and Lebanon, and we will continue to press forward toward that goal.

On the Palestinian front, Israelis and Palestinians are confronting core issues that have defined their conflict for the past fifty years, seeking to build a lasting peace based on partnership and cooperation. Although the July 2000 summit at Camp David failed to achieve a permanent status agreement and violence has recently erupted in the West Bank and Gaza, the United States will continue its efforts to assist both sides in their search for a lasting and just peace. Our goal remains the normalization of relations between Israel and all Arab states. Through the multilateral working groups on security, refugees, water, and the environment, we are seeking to promote regional cooperation to address transboundary environmental issues that affect all parties.

North Africa

The United States has an interest in the stability and prosperity of North Africa, a region that is undergoing important changes. In particular, we are seeking to strengthen our relations with Morocco, Tunisia, and Algeria, and to encourage democratic development and economic reform. Libya continues to be a country of concern for the national security and foreign policy interests of the United States. Although the government of Libya has taken an important positive step away from its support of terrorism by surrendering the Lockerbie suspects, our policy toward Libya is designed to encourage Libya to completely cease its support of terrorism and to block its efforts to obtain weapons of mass destruction.

Southwest Asia

In Southwest Asia, the United States remains focused on deterring threats to regional stability and energy security, countering threats posed by WMD, and protecting the security of our regional partners, particularly from the threats posed by Iraq and Iran. We will continue to encourage members of the Gulf Cooperation Council (GCC) to work closely on collective defense and security arrangements, help individual GCC states meet their defense requirements, and maintain our bilateral defense relationships. For example, the United States is fostering counterproliferation cooperation with, and among, the GCC states through the Cooperative Defense Initiative.

We will maintain an appropriate military presence in Southwest Asia using a combination of ground, air, and naval forces. The terrorist attack on the USS Cole has not deterred our resolve to maintain a continuous military presence in the Gulf to enhance regional stability and defend against threats to friendly countries. Our forces in the Gulf are backed by our ability to rapidly reinforce the region in time of crisis, which we have demonstrated convincingly. We remain committed to the UN Security Council resolutions and preventing the Iraqi regime from taking large-scale military action against Kuwait or the Kurd and Shia minorities in Iraq.

Our policy toward Iraq is comprised of three central elements: containment to prevent Saddam from again threatening the stability of the vital Gulf region; relief for the Iraqi people via the UN oil-for-food program; and support to those Iraqis seeking to replace Saddam's regime with a government that can live at peace with its neighbors and its people.

Containment of Iraq remains the foundation of our policy toward Saddam Hussein's regime. Until his government can be removed from power, it must be prevented from again threatening the region. In December 1999, the United Nations Security Council passed UNSCR 1284, a new omnibus resolution on Iraq. The United States supports Resolution 1284 because it buttresses the containment of Iraq while maximizing relief for the Iraqi people. The resolution expands the humanitarian aspects of the oil-for-food program to ensure the well being of the Iraqi people. It provides for a robust new inspection and monitoring regime that would finish the work begun by UNSCOM. It would allow for a suspension of the economic sanctions in return for full Iraqi cooperation with UN arms inspections and Iraqi fulfillment of key disarmament tasks. This resolution would also lock in the Security Council's control over Iraqi finances to ensure that Saddam Hussein is never again able to disburse Iraq's resources as he would like.

Although Iraq continues to refuse to implement any of the requirements of Resolution 1284, the United States and other members of the Security Council have already begun to implement those sections of the resolution intended to improve the humanitarian situation of the Iraqi populace. Iraqi oil exports have increased dramatically, making possible the procurement of ever-larger quantities of humanitarian necessities. In addition, the Security Council has greatly expanded the lists of items that Iraq is allowed to import to include educational supplies, building materials, spare parts for the oil industry, infrastructure necessities, and other economic goods.

Nevertheless, we consistently maintain that sanctions on Iraq can only be lifted after it has met its obligations to the international community in full. Saddam's actions over the past decade lead us to conclude that his regime will never comply with the obligations contained in the relevant UN Security Council resolutions. For this reason, we actively support those who seek to bring a new democratic government to power in Baghdad. We recognize that this may be a slow and difficult process, but we believe it is the only solution to the problem of Saddam's regime.

Our policy toward Iran is aimed at changing the practices of the Iranian government in several key areas, including its efforts to obtain WMD and long-range missiles, its support for terrorism and groups that violently oppose the Middle East peace process, and its human rights practices. We view signs of change in Iranian policies with great interest, both with regard to the possibility of Iran assuming its rightful place in the world community and the chance for better bilateral ties. We welcome statements by some Iranian officials that advocate improved relations with the United States.

These positive signs must be balanced against the reality that Iran's support for terrorism has not yet ceased and serious violations of human rights persist. Iran is continuing its efforts to acquire WMD and develop long range missiles (including the 1,300 kilometer-range Shahab-3 it flight-tested in July 1998, July 2000, and again in September 2000). The United States will continue to oppose Iranian efforts to sponsor terrorism and to oppose transfers from any country to Iran of materials and technologies that could be used to develop long-range missiles or WMD. Additionally, the United States will continue to work with Arab allies threatened by WMD to develop a defense through efforts such as the Cooperative Defense Initiative.

The United States has demonstrated that we are ready to explore ways to build mutual confidence and avoid misunderstandings with Iran. In recognition of the positive changes in Iran, in particular the fair and free parliamentary elections of February 2000, we modified our sanctions to allow Iran to export to the United States carpets and foodstuffs -- key exports for small Iranian businesses and to facilitate people to people contact. We would welcome reciprocal steps from Iran, and continue to signal our willingness to engage in an authoritative government-to-government dialogue in which both sides will be able to discuss their issues of concern.

Meanwhile, we will strengthen our cooperation with allies and friends to encourage further positive changes in Iranian practices that threaten our shared interests. If a government-to-government dialogue can be initiated and sustained in a way that addresses the concerns of both sides, then the United States would be willing to develop with the Islamic Republic a road map leading to normal relations. It could be useful to begin a dialogue without preconditions.

South Asia

The President's trip to South Asia in March 2000 reflected the growing importance of the region to U.S. political, economic, and commercial interests. As the President emphasized, our strategy for South Asia is designed to help the peoples of that region by helping resolve long-standing conflicts, encouraging economic development, and assisting social development. Regional stability and improved bilateral ties are also important for U.S. economic interests in a region that contains one-fifth of the world's population and one of its most important emerging markets. In addition, we seek to work closely with regional countries to stem the flow of illegal drugs from South Asia, most notably from Afghanistan.

The President stressed the importance we place on reconciliation between India and Pakistan and our encouragement of direct dialogue between them to resolve all their outstanding problems. He urged also that they respect the Line of Control in Kashmir, reject violence as a means to settle their dispute, and exercise mutual restraint.

We seek to establish relationships with India and Pakistan that are defined in terms of their own individual merits and reflect the full range of U.S. strategic, political and economic interests in each country. After the President's visit to India, we are working to enhance our relationship with India at all levels. We look forward to more frequent high-level contacts including meetings between our heads of government and our cabinet officials. With Pakistan, a long-standing friend with which we seek improved relations, we are constrained by the lack of a democratic government since the October 1999 military coup. We have urged Pakistan's leaders to quickly restore civilian rule and the democratic process. The President's visit to Islamabad signified our intent to stay engaged with Pakistan and work to promote that return to democracy.

We seek, as part of our dialogue with India and Pakistan, to encourage both countries to take steps to prevent further proliferation, reduce the risk of conflict, and exercise restraint in their nuclear and missile programs. The United States does not believe that nuclear weapons have made India or Pakistan more secure. We hope they will abandon their nuclear weapons programs and join the NPT as non-nuclear weapon states. Indian and Pakistani nuclear and long-range missile tests have been dangerously destabilizing and threaten to spark a dangerous arms race in South Asia. Such a race will further undermine the global nonproliferation regime and thus threaten international security.

In concert with the other permanent members of the UN Security Council, the G-8 nations, and many others in the international community, the United States has called on India and Pakistan to take a number of steps that would bring them closer to the international mainstream on nonproliferation. These include: signing and ratifying the Comprehensive Nuclear Test Ban Treaty, joining the clear international consensus in support of a cutoff of fissile material production, strengthening export controls, and refraining from an arms race in nuclear weapons and long-range missiles. We have also urged them to resume their direct dialogue and take decisive steps to reduce tensions in South Asia. In that regard, we have urged India and Pakistan to agree to a multilateral moratorium on the production of fissile material, pending the conclusion of a Fissile Materials Cutoff Treaty (FIVICT).

Afghanistan remains a serious threat to U.S. worldwide interests because of the Taliban's continued sheltering of international terrorists and its increasing export of illicit drugs. Afghanistan remains the primary safehaven for terrorists threatening the United States, including Usama bin Ladin. The United Nations and the United States have levied sanctions against the Taliban for harboring Usama bin Ladin and other terrorists, and will continue to pressure the Taliban until it complies with international requests to bring bin Ladin to justice. The United States remains concerned about those countries, including Pakistan, that support the Taliban and allow it to continue to harbor such radical elements. We are engaged in energetic diplomatic efforts, including through the United Nations and with Russia and other concerned countries, to address these concerns on an urgent basis.

Promoting Prosperity

The United States has two principal economic objectives in the region: to promote regional economic cooperation and development, and to ensure an unrestricted flow of oil from the region. We seek to promote regional trade and cooperation on infrastructure through the peace process and our Qualifying Industrial Zone program, which provides economic benefits for certain countries that enter into business arrangements with Israel. In South Asia, we will continue to work with the region's countries in their efforts to implement market reforms, strengthen educational systems, and end the use of child and sweatshop labor.

Although the United States imports less than 15% of the oil exported from the Persian Gulf, the region will remain of vital strategic importance to U.S. national security due to the global nature of the international oil market. Previous oil shocks and the Gulf War underscore that any blockage of Gulf supplies or sudden changes in price would immediately affect the international market, driving up energy costs everywhere -- ultimately harming the U.S. economy as well as the economies of our key economic partners in Europe and Asia. Appropriate responses to events such as Iraq's invasion of Kuwait can limit the magnitude of a crisis in the Gulf and its impact on world oil markets. Over the longer term, U.S. dependence on access to these and other foreign oil sources will remain important as our reserves are depleted. That is one of many important reasons why the United States must continue to demonstrate commitment and resolve in the Persian Gulf. We will continue our regular dialogue with the oil-producing nations to ensure a safe supply of oil and stable prices.

Promoting Democracy and Human Rights

We encourage the spread of democratic values throughout the Middle East, North Africa and Southwest and South Asia and will pursue this objective aided by constructive dialogue with countries in the region. In Iran, for example, we hope the nation's leaders will carry out the people's mandate for a government that respects and protects the rule of law, both in its internal and external affairs. In Pakistan, we have pressed the new military rulers to provide a detailed roadmap with a timetable for a return to elected civilian government. In India, during the President's visit, we supported the establishment of an Asian Center for Democratic Governance, which would seek to promote the forms and substance of democracy throughout Asia. We will promote responsible indigenous moves toward increasing political participation and enhancing the quality of governance, and we will continue to challenge governments in the region to improve their human rights records. We will work with the governments and human rights organizations of the region to promote tolerance for the diverse religious groups present in the Middle East and South Asia. In particular, we have sought to encourage and end to violence against minority religious groups, and a repeal of "blasphemy laws" which are used to discriminate against minorities.

Respect for human rights also requires rejection of terrorism. If the nations in the region are to safeguard their own citizens from the threat of terror, they cannot tolerate acts of indiscriminate violence against civilians, nor can they offer refuge to those who commit such acts. We will continue to enforce UNSC sanctions against the Taliban for harboring terrorists such as Usama bin Ladin and look for other ways to pressure the Taliban to end its support for such groups.

Our policies are guided by our profound respect for Islam. The Muslim religion is the fastest-growing faith in the United States. We recognize and honor Islam's role as a source of inspiration, instruction, and moral guidance for hundreds of millions of people around the world. United States policy in the region is directed at the actions of governments and terrorist groups, not peoples or faiths.

Sub-Saharan Africa

In recent years, the United States has engaged in a concerted effort to transform our relationship with Africa. We have supported efforts by many African nations to move toward multi-party democracy, hold free and fair elections, promote human rights, allow freedom of the press and association, enhance civil and judicial institutions, and reform their economies. A new, post-Cold War political order is emerging in Africa, with emphasis on democratic and pragmatic approaches to solving political, economic, and environmental problems, and developing human and natural resources. United States-Africa ties are deepening, and U.S.-Africa trade is expanding.

Sustaining these recent successes will require that we identify those issues that most directly affect our interests. We will promote regional stability through engagement with sub-regional organizations and key African states using carefully harmonized U.S. programs and initiatives. We recognize and are sensitive to the challenges many African states face as they move toward multi-party democracy and civil-military relations, and we will work to focus our limited resources on assisting their transition. Our immediate objective is to increase the number of capable states in Africa, that is, nations that are able to define the challenges they face, manage their resources to effectively address those challenges, and build stability and peace within their borders and their sub-regions.

Enhancing Security

Serious transnational security threats emanate from pockets of Africa, including state-sponsored terrorism, drug trafficking and other international crime, environmental degradation, and infectious diseases, especially HIV/AIDS. Since these threats transcend state borders, they are best addressed through effective, sustained sub-regional engagement in Africa. We have already made some progress in countering some of these threats -- such as by investing in efforts to combat environmental degradation and infectious disease, and leading international efforts to remove mines planted in previous conflict areas and halt the proliferation of land mines. We continue efforts to reduce the flow of illegal drugs through Africa and to curtail international organized criminal activity based in Africa. We will improve international intelligence sharing, and train and assist African law enforcement, intelligence, and border control agencies to detect and prevent planned terrorist attacks against U.S. targets in Africa.

We seek to keep Africa free of weapons of mass destruction by supporting South Africa's nuclear disarmament and accession to the NPT as a non-nuclear weapon state, supporting the African Nuclear Weapons Free Zone, and encouraging African nations to join the BWC and CWC.

Nigeria's rapid change from an autocratic, military regime to a civilian, democratically elected government has afforded us the opportunity to build a promising security, political and economic relationship with the most populous country in Africa. With nearly one in six Africans living in Nigeria, the impact of serious cooperative efforts to tackle significant drug trafficking, corruption, and other crime could be enormously beneficial to the United States and a large proportion of Africans. In Sierra Leone, we are working with West Africa -- particularly Nigeria -- the United Kingdom, and the UN to prevent the spread of conflict, promote accountability, and deal with the role of diamonds in financing the rebels. We are also seeking to establish the control of a democratically elected government over the national territory. Additionally, we are addressing the role of diamonds and the proliferation of small arms in fueling conflicts in Angola, the Democratic Republic of the Congo, and elsewhere. In the Democratic Republic of the Congo and Angola, where fighting threatens to destabilize a broad swath of central and southern Africa, we are working closely with the region and the UN to support the Lusaka peace process. Similarly, we have provided significant political support to the Arusha Peace Process to bring a resolution to the ongoing conflict in Burundi. We have also been working closely with the UN and Organization for African Unity (OAU) to attempt to establish a lasting peace between Ethiopia and Eritrea.

Sudan continues to pose a threat to regional stability and the national security interests of the United States. We have moved to counter Sudan's support for international terrorism and regional destabilization by maintaining the sanctions imposed against the Khartoum regime until it takes concrete, verifiable steps to end support for terrorism on Sudanese soil; we continue to press for the regime's isolation through the UN Security Council. We support regional efforts for a just and fair peace and national reconciliation in Sudan based on the Inter-Governmental Authority on Development's Declaration of Principles.

Persistent conflict and continuing political instability in some African countries remain obstacles to Africa's development and to our national security, political and economic interests there, including assured access to oil reserves and other important natural resources. To foster regional stability and peace in Africa, the United States in 1996 launched the African Crisis Response Initiative (ACRI) to train African militaries to conduct effective peacekeeping and humanitarian operations. It will focus on developing a sustainable regional capacity to address the multiple challenges to peace and security on the continent. We are consulting closely on expanded ACRI activity with the UN Department of Peacekeeping Operations, the OAU and its Crisis Management Center, and African sub-regional organizations already pursuing similar capability enhancements. A different effort, Operation Focus Relief, is training and equipping seven West African battalions for peace enforcement missions in Sierra Leone. And finally, another initiative, the Enhanced International Peacekeeping Capabilities (EIPC) program, provides funding to upgrade peacekeeping and training centers, and "train the trainer' in countries around the world in order to make them more interoperable with U.S. and other peacekeeping forces, thereby sharing the burden.

The United States has established the Africa Center for Strategic Studies (ACSS) to promote the exchange of ideas and information tailored specifically for African security concerns. The goal is for ACSS to be a source of academic, yet practical, instruction in promoting civil-military relations and the skills necessary to make effective national security decisions in democratic governments. The curriculum will engage African military and civilian defense leaders in a substantive dialogue about defense policy planning, civil-military relations, and defense resource management in democracies. Our long-term goal is to support the development of regional security arrangements and institutions to prevent and manage armed conflicts and curtail transnational threats to our collective security.

Promoting Prosperity

A stable, democratic, prosperous Africa will be a better economic partner, a better partner for security and peace, and a better partner in the fights against drug trafficking, crime, terrorism, infectious diseases, and environmental degradation. Lasting prosperity for Africa will be possible only when Africa is fully integrated into the global economy.

Further integrating Africa into the global economy will also directly serve U.S. interests by continuing to expand an already important new market for U.S. exports. The approximately 700 million people of sub-Saharan Africa represent one of the world's largest basically untapped markets. Although the United States enjoys only a 7% market share in Africa, already 100,000 American jobs depend on our exports there. Increasing both the U.S. market share and the size of the African market will bring tangible benefits to U.S. workers and increase prosperity and economic opportunity in Africa. Our aim, therefore, is to assist African nations to implement economic reforms, improve public governance and combat corruption, create favorable climates for trade and investment, and achieve sustainable development.

To support the economic transformation underway in Africa, the President in June 1997 launched the Partnership for Economic Growth and Opportunity in Africa Initiative. The Administration has implemented many of the Initiative's objectives and continues to work closely with Congress to implement remaining key elements of this initiative. The enactment of the African Growth and Opportunity Act on May 18, 2000 marked the beginning of a new relationship between the United States and sub-Saharan Africa. This legislation provides the opportunity for substantial preferential market access to the U.S. market for eligible sub-Saharan African countries, and provides an economic, human rights, and civil-judicial benchmark towards which current non-eligible countries can aspire and focus their development efforts.

By significantly broadening market access, spurring growth, and helping the poorest nations eliminate or reduce their bilateral debt, the Initiative and the legislation better enable us to help African nations undertake difficult economic reforms and build better lives for their people through sustainable development. We are working with African governments on shared interests in the world trading system, such as developing electronic commerce, improving WTO capacity-building functions, and eliminating agricultural export subsidies. We also are pursuing initiatives to encourage U.S. trade with and investment in Africa, including targeted technical assistance, enhanced debt forgiveness, and increased bilateral trade ties.

To further our trade objectives in Africa, the Ron Brown Commercial Center was established in Johannesburg, South Africa in 1998. The Center provides support for American companies looking to enter or expand into the sub-Saharan African market, promotes U.S. exports through a range of support programs, and facilitates business contacts and partnerships between African and American businesses. The President's historic March 1998 trip to Africa and the unprecedented March 1999 U.S.-Africa Ministerial further solidified our partnership with African nations across a range of security, economic, and political issues.

Helping Africans generate the food and income necessary to feed themselves is critical for promoting sustainable growth and development. Despite some recent progress, the percentage of malnourished people and lack of diversified sustainable agricultural production in Africa is the highest of any region in the world, and more help is greatly needed. In 1998 we launched the Africa Food Security Initiative (AFSI), a USAID-led effort to help improve agricultural productivity, support research, expand income-generating projects, and address nutritional needs for the rural poor. While maintaining its program focus in the original AFSI countries -- Ethiopia, Mali, Mozambique, Malawi, and Uganda -- the initiative is now being expanded into countries where food security is declining, such as Tanzania and Zambia, as well as Ghana and Kenya, where we can build on other USAID programs to accelerate our goals of improved child nutrition and increased agricultural incomes.

The initial focus under the AFSI involved countries that were either on the fast growth track or countries that had undertaken a degree of structural adjustment that would put them on the right path. Ethiopia, Mali, Mozambique, Malawi, and Uganda, the initial focus countries, have performed reasonably well under the circumstances. Productivity and agriculture incomes had been rising before the floods in southern Africa or the drought in East Africa. All of these countries either met or exceeded their performance targets last year. Food grants production per capita, one of the Initiative's objectives, has continued its upward trend last year. Of these countries, all except Ethiopia -- whose war with Eritrea has continued during this period -- are showing improving food security trends.

However, the picture is less encouraging in much of Africa. Malnutrition accounts for about one-third of all children's deaths in Africa. And although there has been a decline in the percentage of preschoolers in Africa who are stunted, the number is going up -- the only place in the world where this is the case -- from about 35 million in 1980 to a projection of 50 million in 2005.

The Africa Food Security Initiative, while maintaining its program focus in the original AFSI countries, is expanding its program into countries where food security is declining, such as Tanzania and Zambia, as well as Ghana and Kenya, where we can build on USAID program to accelerate our goals of improved child nutrition and increased agriculture incomes.

USAID has been able to make progress on the Initiative by focusing on working with governments to improve agricultural policies, working with farmers and researchers to increase the technologies that allow for yield increases (or cut production costs), and working with farmer groups to improve their ability to market their produce more competitively. We are also working closely with African partners to make available usable technologies such as air traffic control systems and other airfield improvements, as well as introducing the U.S. Army Corps of Engineers to provide training and demonstration projects.

African nations are also engaged in battle with age-old diseases, such as malaria and tuberculosis (TB), which sap economic productivity and development. Worse, the epidemic of HIV/AIDS is devastating the continent, reversing hard-fought gains in development, dramatically reducing life expectancy, decreasing GDPs, and threatening security and stability in the hardest-hit nations. The Administration has made the battle against AIDS and other diseases a priority for international action and investment in Africa. Over the past two years, the President has doubled bilateral assistance for the fight against HIV/AIDS, launched the Millennium Vaccine Initiative to accelerate the search for vaccines against HIV/AIDS, malaria, and TB, and launched a campaign to mobilize new resources from other donors, such as the G-8, and the private sector. We have also begun the Leadership in Fighting an Epidemic (LIFE) initiative, a $100 million effort with legislative backing, which focuses on training and prevention activities for selected sub-Saharan African militaries.

Promoting Democracy and Human Rights

In Africa as elsewhere, democracies have proved to be stronger partners for peace, stability and sustained prosperity. We will continue to support the important progress African nations have achieved and to broaden the growing circle of African democracies.

The restoration of civilian democratic government in Nigeria can help return that country to its place as a leader in Africa. The government and people of Nigeria have succeeded in restoring democratic civilian government, freed political prisoners, lifted onerous restrictions on labor unions, and worked to restore the authority of the judicial system. Nigeria's new civilian government has taken sweeping steps to ensure that the military remains in the barracks and that fighting corruption will be a top priority. The peaceful elections in February 1999 and inauguration of the new civilian government in May 1999 were important steps in this transformation.

As in any democratic transition, Nigeria's new government is facing enormous challenges: creating accountable government, building support within the military for civilian rule, protecting human rights, and rebuilding the economy so it benefits all citizens. President Clinton met with President Obasanjo at the White House in October 1999 and again in Nigeria in August 2000. The discussions reaffirmed our nation's commitment to work with him on the security, economic, political, and social challenges faced by Nigeria. Kenya, which has played a critical role in maintaining regional stability, is also facing an historic transition. President Daniel Moi has announced that he will step down in 2002, after twenty-four years in power. He leaves a country that is suffering from a weak economy and deteriorating social infrastructure. We must continue to actively engage the Government of Kenya on such matters as conflict resolution, regional stability, and economic development as well as encouraging commitment to constitutional reform and human rights.

Democracy assistance has proven to be an effective tool in both Senegal and Zimbabwe. In Senegal, President Abdou Diouf accepted defeat in the March elections and turned power over peacefully to Abdoulaye Wade, the opposition leader. The most recent elections had a record high voter turnout of educated voters despite several complicating factors. In order to help post-apartheid South Africa achieve its economic, political, democratic, and security goals for all its citizens, we will continue to provide substantial bilateral assistance, vigorously promote U.S. trade and investment, and pursue close cooperation and support for our mutual interests.

Ultimately, the prosperity and security of Africa depend on African leadership, strong national institutions, and extensive political and economic reform. The United States will continue to support and promote such national reforms and the evolution of regional arrangements that build cooperation among African states.

IV. Conclusions

Over the last eight years, we have once again mustered the creative energies of our Nation to reestablish the United States' military and economic strength within the world community. This leadership position has been achieved in a manner in which our forefathers would likely have been pleased; a nation leading by the authority that comes from the attractiveness of its values and force of its example, rather than the power of its military might to compel by force or sanction. As a result, the world now looks to the United States to be not just a broker of peace, but a catalyst of coalitions, and a guarantor of global financial stability. It has been achieved in spite of a period of tumultuous change in the strategic landscape. Yet, it has been realized because we have maintained a steadfast focus on simple goals -- peace, shared prosperity, and freedom -- that lift the condition of all nations and people that choose to join us.

Our strategy for engagement is comprised of many different policies, the key elements of which include:

- Adapting our alliances

- Encouraging the reorientation of other states, including former adversaries

- Encouraging democratization, open markets, free trade, and sustainable development

- Preventing conflict

- Countering potential regional aggressors

- Confronting new threats

- Steering international peace and stability operations.

These elements are building blocks within a strategic architecture that describe a foreign policy for a global age. They are not easily summed up in a single phrase but they have all been guided by two simple principles -- protecting our interests and advancing our values. Together, the sum of these goals, elements, and principles represent the blueprint for our strategy of engagement, and we believe that strategy will best achieve our vision for the future.

But we must not be too sanguine about the future. New challenges to the sustainability of our current economic, political, and national security successes will arise. The true question is what will best ensure our leadership in the years ahead. It took great vision almost a decade ago to realize that strength abroad would depend not only on maintaining an internationalist philosophy but also on reestablishing strength at home. Putting our economic house in order, while not retreating into isolationism proved a wise course and validated the mutual linkage between disparate goals of peace, shared prosperity, and democracy. Any other policy choice might well have permitted the world to fall into a series of regional conflicts in the aftermath of the Cold War and possibly have precluded opportunity for the U.S. economic recovery of the 1990s. Although past is not necessarily prologue, the inexorable trend of globalization supports the continued viability of a strategy of engagement. We must not, in reaction to the real or perceived costs of engagement, retreat into a policy of "Fortress America." To do so would lead us down a path that would dishonor our commitments, ignore our friends, and discount belief in our values. The result would be a global loss of our authority and with it ultimately our power. A strategy of engagement, however, is the surest way to enhance not only our power but also our authority, and thus our leadership, into the 21st century.

www.ingramcontent.com/pod-product-compliance
Lightning Source LLC
Chambersburg PA
CBHW080320290526

45790CB00005B/2121